Critical Praise for Quiet Places of Massachusetts

"The measure of Tougias' talent is his ability to let the reader see through newly opened eyes. He shows nature and place through a magic glass, from a new angle." *Springfield Union*

"Tougias writes in a clear, down-to-earth style." *Boston Globe*

"Different from other travel books in that it's a little bit travel, a little bit history, and a little bit personal diary." *Dartmouth Chronicle*

"An interesting and charming book where Tougias writes free and poetic. He recounts his experiences in a concise and welcoming way." *The Standard Times*

D0896781

Hunter Publishing, Inc.
300 Raritan Center Parkway
Edison NJ 08818, USA
Tel (908) 225 1900
Fax (908) 417 0482

164 Commander Boulevard
Agincourt, Ontario
CANADA M15 3C7
Tel (416) 293 8141

ISBN 1-55650-729-1

© 1996 Michael J. Tougias

All rights reserved. No part of this publication may be reproduced, stored in a retrieval system, or transmitted in any form, or by any means, electronic, mechanical, photocopying, recording, or otherwise, without the written permission of the publisher.

Every effort has been made to ensure that the information in this book is correct, but the publisher and authors do not assume, and hereby disclaim, any liability to any party for any loss or damage caused by errors, omissions, misleading information or any potential problem caused by information in this guide, even if these are a result of negligence, accident or any other cause.

Maps by Kim André

Cover photo by author
Sketches by Mark Tougias

Quiet Places

of

Massachusetts

Country rambles, secluded beaches, backroad
excursions, romantic retreats

Michael J. Tougias

Acknowledgements

Books are born in strange ways; you cannot force them, you cannot rush them. QUIET PLACES was the result of a chance encounter. In 1994 I was attending the New England Booksellers Association annual convention when I met Michael Hunter, president of Hunter Publishing. We fell into converstaion, and I explained how I'd been knocking about the back roads in search of quiet places. One thing led to another and within 20 minutes we had an idea for a book that appealed to both of us.

During the final year of writing, it was Michael's enthusiastic words about the chapters I had sent him that helped the project along. No book had ever gone quite so smoothly, and I have to believe QUIET PLACES had a mind of its own, waiting for the right publisher to bring it to fruition. And maybe, just maybe, QUIET PLACES will inspire others to save more of earth's natural treasures.

About the Author

Michael Tougias is a native New Englander who writes on a wide range of topics, including history, nature, gardening, and travel. His columns appear in the *Springfield Union News, The Patriot Ledger, The Middlesex News, The Sun Chronicle* and other newspapers. In his free time he enjoys hiking with his family, fishing, canoeing, and reading. When not exploring Massachusetts, he spends time at his rustic cabin in northern Vermont.

Tougias frequently gives slide presentations about special historic and natural places in New England. Whenever possible he volunteers for conservation work in an effort to save more open spaces. He is the author of *Nature Walks in Eastern Massachusetts, The Hidden Charles, Country Roads of Massachusetts, Nature Walks in Central Massachusetts, Autumn Trails,* and *A Taunton River Journey.* His first novel, *Until I Have No Country,* is an historic work of King Philip's Indian War. It will be released in fall of 1996. He has also published Recreation Maps and Guides to *Cape Cod, Hidden Quabbin,* and the *Southern Berkshires.* If you are interested in his publications or slide presentations, send a self-addressed stamped envelope to M. Tougias, PO Box 72, Norfolk, MA 02056.

Contents

Maps

Foreword

This book and the research (mostly fun rambles through the countryside and visits to local libraries) was done over a period of two years. The format is a little unusual, combining practical travel information with personal experiences and feelings I had while visiting these special places. This style is intended to appeal to both the active explorer and the armchair traveler.

I envision some readers using the book with pen in hand, circling the places that particularly speak to them, luring them to the open road. Nature lovers will find stories of unusual wildlife encounters, and those interested in history will learn of some lesser-known events that took place off the beaten path. I hope these will surprise you.

Come with me on an exploration of my home state's quiet places, and return with a fresh sense of the wonder and beauty of life.

To those special friends who make life's
journey so much richer

Western Massachusetts

Massachusetts

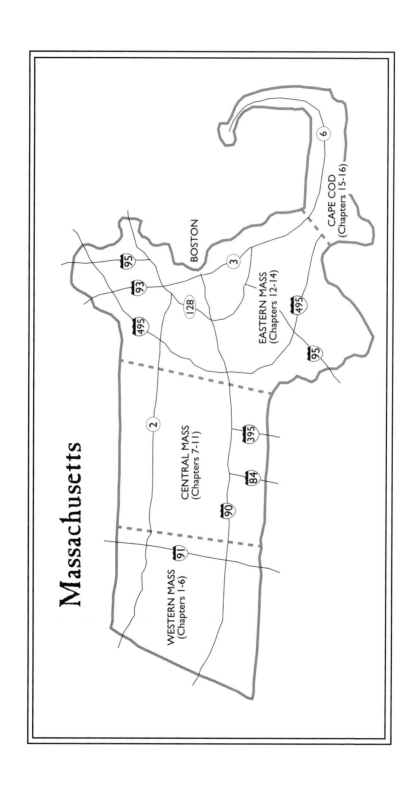

BOSTON

95

93

495

128

3

EASTERN MASS
(Chapters 12-14)

495

95

CAPE COD
(Chapters 15-16)

6

2

CENTRAL MASS
(Chapters 7-11)

395

84

90

91

WESTERN MASS
(Chapters 1-6)

The Northern Berkshires & Hill Towns

Florida, Monroe, Charlemont, West Hawley, Plainfield, Cummington & Goshen

On a warm October morning – a real Indian summer – my brother Mark and I followed the **Deerfield River** northward, far off the beaten path and into the isolated mountain town of **Florida**. This is a far cry from the Sunshine State, and not exactly a tourist spot. You won't find Disney World, Busch Gardens or beaches here, but hikers and nature lovers should make it a point to explore this area, as the rewards are many. Especially interesting is the **Dunbar Brook Trail**, owned by the New England Power Company. That is where Mark and I began our morning jaunt.

The trail follows the brook upstream from its confluence with the Deerfield River, climbing into rugged, wooded hills. Right away I knew I was going to like the place. Instead of the pines and oaks that dominate the area around my home in southeastern Massachusetts, we found massive hemlocks, maples, and white birch – as close to the "forest primeval" as I've ever seen. And the brook was a classic mountain stream, surging down the hills, flexing its muscles.

Scenery like this gives your legs their own special energy, and the rhythm of walking was like music. The farther upstream we ventured, the more rugged the land became, with little waterfalls dropping into slick pools below. Beneath the cathedral of trees, ferns grew in the shade – deep green over a blanket of fallen brown leaves. I wondered if Mohawk or Hoosac Indians had once used this same ridge trail.

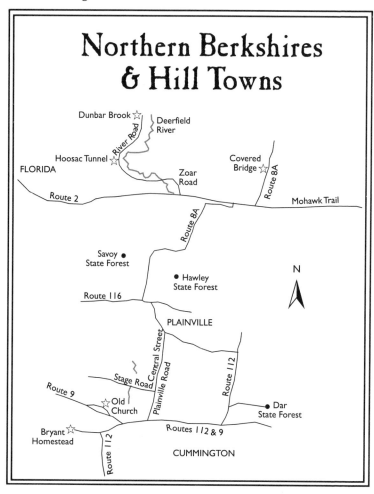

Just after we crossed a log bridge to the opposite side of the stream, Mark spotted an old millstone in the river. I was surprised to learn that early settlers had lived here, in this wild land. But in the 17th and 18th centuries, water-power was a valuable commodity; both grist and lumber mills were erected all along the Commonwealth's rivers and streams.

We didn't find any more evidence of the mill, but five minutes farther up the trail we came upon an old cellar hole. We wondered if this marked the remains of an isolated home, or had there been a little village here that the forest had since swallowed up? It must have been a tough life working this bony land, but to have a home within earshot of the tumbling brook would be wonderful compensation.

Beyond the cellar hole, Dunbar Brook cascades down a series of ledges carved by centuries of falling water, fanning out at the bottom into a wide pool. This is where we finally rested, eating the sandwiches we had packed. The finest restaurant in the state could not duplicate the wonderful taste of those sandwiches; it was the air, the smell of evergreens, and the rigorous walk that made this meal special.

We lay back on the rocks watching the last of the leaves drop from the beech and maples. When the sun went behind a cloud, the wind kicked up, sending an orange avalanche of leaves tumbling down the hill behind us. Now there was a bite to the air, reminding us of the harsher weather soon to come. We shouldered our knapsacks and headed back downstream.

Back in the car, we passed the dark and forbidding entrance of the **Hoosac Tunnel**. Completed in 1876, this railroad tunnel took a monumental 25 years to build. It travels four and a half miles straight through the mountain. I could only imagine the conditions the laborers endured during its construction.

It was near the tunnel that we surprised a flock of wild turkeys. Though large birds, they're very quick on foot – too quick for my camera. In all my years of hiking the Bay State, these were the first wild turkeys I had seen. But they may not be the last, since their population is on the increase.

The turkey was Benjamin Franklin's nominee for the United States national bird. If you're only familiar with fat farm turkeys, you might wonder if old Ben was serious. But the wild turkey is a different bird altogether; he's faster, more cautious, and capable of flight.

Later, Mark and I explored some of the town's backroads. One was so steep that we could only climb it in first gear. On the descent, our ears popped as though we were landing a jet. We also came across a forlorn cemetery on a wooded hilltop. I remarked that perhaps 100 years ago there was a thriving village nearby. "Who knows, maybe in the next 100 years this will be suburbia," Mark said. I shuddered at the thought – we've already seen what development did to the *other* Florida.

Next, we followed the Deerfield River southward, stopping to fly-fish at a couple of "secret holes." Many anglers regard the Deerfield as Massachusetts' best trout stream, and I have to agree. This was one of the first rivers in the state to have a catch-and-release section, and the experiment has been a success. The result is bigger trout, and more of them.

The stretches of whitewater also attract the attention of experienced canoeists, kayakers, and rafters. And for those who have never run the rapids, there are outfitters – such as **Zoar Outdoors** and **Crab Apple Whitewater** – that rent equipment, provide lessons, and offer guided excursions on the river.

I try to avoid Route 2, The Mohawk Trail, because the traffic moves too quickly for a slow-poke like me. (Of course, it can get very crowded during October, when the leaf-peepers are out.) So Mark and I turned onto Route 8A, first heading north one-fifth of a mile to see one of the region's more scenic covered bridges. Large log railings line the edge of the road, directing your eye to the weather-worn boards of the **Bissell Bridge**. There are windows inside; it is possible to look out and see the Mill River passing below. Years ago, a bridge such as this would have been the perfect spot for a young couple to park their wagon for a bit of sparkin'.

Bissell Bridge was built in 1951 at the site of another covered bridge that once carried wagons to a nearby iron mine. When the new bridge was completed, the town of **Charlemont** held a square dance on it to celebrate the occasion!

There are a number of theories about why so many bridges were covered in the 1800s and the early 1900s. Most of these center around horses, because the bridges were built before the age of the automobile. It is said that horses feared crossing water at a height, and by covering a bridge the horses would get the impression they were simply entering a barn. The bridges also offered protection for horse, driver and wagons of hay during sudden summer downpours. Still another theory has it that the bridges were covered to prevent horses from slipping on the smooth wooden planking during periods of ice and snow.

But the real reason for covering a bridge has nothing to do with horses. Instead, it relates to the structure itself. Wood exposed to the elements decays faster than wood that is protected, and a roof shelters the bridge's important structural members in the span. Periodic replacement of the roof would be far simpler than repairing the timbers below.

Mark and I stopped here, taking pictures and examining the bridge's construction. Visiting a covered bridge can take you back to a simpler time. As we sat quietly by the river, I could almost hear the squeak of wagon wheels and the thud of hoofs on the wooden planks.

Bissell Bridge

Heading south on 8A, we soon passed the wilds of the **Savoy and Hawley State Forests**. This is an isolated, rugged region, with only a handful of homes and an unmarked church hugging the hillsides. The road was most memorable for the rough-legged hawk that flew by with a snake in its talons. We searched the woods for bears, knowing this part of Massachusetts has more black bears than any other.

We also wondered if the "ghost of the forest," the mountain lion, was living nearby. Though these creatures are considered extinct in New England, reports of cougar sightings persist – especially here in the Berkshire Hills and the woods of Quabbin. On my last visit to the region, I met a man who said he saw a lion cross the Cold River, just a few miles from here. Count me as one of the believers. If there are cougars roaming these forests, it's unclear whether they were illegally released from captivity or are truly wild. It's also uncertain whether or not there is a breeding population. But it's possible; there are certainly enough deer to support them.

We passed through the sleepy village of **Plainville** and turned onto **Central Street**, a fine old country road lined by ancient maples, woods and fields.

Then Mark and I stopped to fish a stream on **Stage Road**, where the water cascades over the remains of an old stone dam at a former mill site. Beaver had made good use of this spot. Their dam of sticks and mud was erected just above the mill site, forming a good-sized pool of water for their protection. From mill pond to beaver pond – I wondered what the former mill owner would have thought.

Two young boys were fishing downstream from us, one of them furiously trying to free his lure from a tree. For a moment I considered going over to give a hand and perhaps offer some casting tips. But then I remembered the last time I gave a couple of youngsters some fishing advice. When I finished telling them about the habits of trout and the best lures to use, one of the boys opened his battered and rusted tackle box to show me something. Crammed inside was a fat brown trout, no less than 16 inches long. I decided to keep my advice to myself.

When we reached Cummington, we followed Route 9 west a couple of miles to **West Cummington**. Here we stopped and took photos of an old church nestled in the woods. It rises above the village and the river below, like a sentinel guarding this peaceful place.

On past trips to the Cummington-Goshen area I've visited the **DAR Forest**. This is a great place for swimming and boating. It also has one of the few firetowers in the state that is open to the public. From the top, there are commanding vistas over the pines and hemlocks that seem to stretch endlessly.

Near the corner of Route 9 and Route 112 South, we stopped at the Creamery Grocery for a drink. Striking up a conversation with one of the locals, I remarked how the dairy farms gave these little towns their special character and open views. But my new friend said the farmers were in trouble, and later research proved him right: Massachusetts has only half the dairy farms it did just 10 years ago. Country life is not always as idyllic as it seems.

From the Creamery Grocery, it's just a couple of miles south on Route 112 to what I consider the perfect home. The 23-room William Cullen Bryant Homestead rests on a hill overlooking rolling countryside and the valley of the Westfield River. A view like this should be enjoyed from a country porch, and this home has a beauty. Maybe that's where the poet and writer Bryant found his peace and inspiration.

This place has an enduring appeal. In 1835, Bryant's widowed mother went into debt and was forced to sell the rambling home. Thirty years later, long after his mother had died, William Cullen Bryant – now a successful poet and newspaper editor – bought it back. Anyone who sees the place will understand why. Cummington could lure anyone back.

If You Go:

Zoar Outdoors	(413) 339-4010
Crab Apple Whitewater	(413) 339-6660
Franklin County Chamber of Commerce	(413) 773-5463
Northern Berkshire Chamber of Commerce	(413) 663-3735
Berkshire Hills Visitors Bureau	(800) 237-5747
Mohawk Trail Association	(413) 458-2767

The **William Cullen Bryant Homestead** is owned by The Trustees of Reservations and is open to the public in the summer and fall. For the latest visiting hours, call (413) 634-2244.

The **Dunbar Brook Hiking Trail** can be reached via River Road near the Florida-Monroe border.

Mount Greylock & the Northwest Berkshires

Williamstown, Adams, North Adams & Lanesborough

On Mothers' Day, 1990, drenching rains pounded **Mount Greylock** in the Berkshires, causing a massive rock slide on the eastern slope. Trees were uprooted, and a large gash of exposed rock became visible as far away as the center of Adams. With most of the trees and brush gone, the profile of a man's face emerged from the granite. It is an angry face, with a mouth twisted downward, jaw jutting forward, high cheekbones and a bald or shaved head with only a lock of hair hanging behind. Many think it resembles an Indian. Perhaps it is Chief Greylock, come back to reclaim his mountain.

At 3,491 feet, Greylock is the highest peak in Massachusetts. The origin of its name is uncertain. Some believe it was named for the dark grey clouds that shroud or "lock" the mountain in winter. But others say it was named after Chief Greylock, a Mohawk leader who lived northwest of the mountain. Now that I've seen the rock slide and its facial profile, I'm inclined to believe the latter story. I like a little mystery.

The rock slide and profile are best seen from Gould Road in Adams. The profile is not easily discernible at a casual glance. One has to know that the face is pointing to the right as you look at it; then it all becomes clear. Perhaps the chief has come back to express his displeasure over encroaching development near the base of the mountain. Perhaps he is reminding us to care for the earth, our common mother.

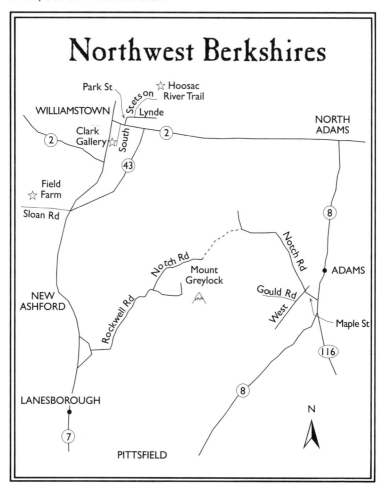

On an early Sunday morning I coaxed my ancient Subaru up the 10-mile access road from Lanesboro. First I climbed through a forest of oak, beech, birch, and hemlocks. Then, after rounding hairpin turns, the trees in the upper elevation changed to mostly conifers (such as red spruce and balsam fir), clinging to the rocky slopes. Periodic views to the west appeared, adding to the sense of exhilaration I get whenever climbing a mountain – whether by foot or by car. Near the summit the trees were smaller, some stunted and twisted from too much wind and not enough soil. Not long ago, much of the mountain was devoid of trees and the east face suffered serious erosion from continual logging.

As my car coughed and growled, I thought of naturalist and author Henry David Thoreau. Even if there had been automobiles in his day, he never would have driven to the top. My guilt increased when I later learned that not only did he blaze his own trail to the summit, he walked here all the way from his home in Concord. Much has been said about Thoreau, but few acknowledge his remarkable physical stamina.

Thoreau's trek to Greylock came at a time when he was going through deep personal doubts. Just a few weeks earlier, he had accidently burned down a vast tract of forest in his native Concord. Perhaps he came to Greylock for escape and contemplation, knowing instinctively that mountains have therapeutic powers.

As great as his stamina was, his planning (or lack of personal concern) left something to be desired. The summit was so cold that he covered himself with boards to ward off the overnight chill. He wrote: "As it grew colder towards midnight, I at length encased myself completely with boards, managing even to put a board on top of me, with a large stone on it to keep it down, and so slept comfortably." I believe the part about the boards, but I'm not so sure about the comfortable sleep.

When I reached the summit, I forgot my guilt about driving up. Here was a sacred place, a cathedral open to the heavens. The 3,491-foot peak has vistas of up to 100 miles, past the Berkshire Hills into the Green Mountains to the north and the rolling hills of New York to the west. The silence was wonderful, but if you stare out from this vantage point long enough you just might hear echos from the past – the chants of Chief Greylock or Thoreau's chattering teeth.

I was so impressed with Mount Greylock and the surrounding hills that I came back the following weekend, taking seven-year-old Kristin with me on our annual father/daughter weekend. We chose **Williamstown** to explore because I'd never been there. It turned out to be a great choice. Williamstown is so handsome and so tastefully laid out that it ranks right up there on my list of most appealing country towns. Located in the northwest corner of the

Berkshires, Williamstown is a small college town, offering the visitor a wide assortment of cultural and outdoor activities.

There is something special about traveling alone with a child in a situation that allows you to give them your full attention. During the ride up, we had great conversations – as if we were long-lost friends, rather than father and daughter. Kristin was asking all sorts of questions, singing with the radio, and simply enjoying the ride. Could it be that the child senses when the adult is relaxed, and responds by opening up?

When we arrived at Williamstown, we took an hour and explored this very walkable town on foot. There were pleasing views in every direction, historic homes, churches, and rolling lawns, all framed by mountains. The campus of Williams College lines the main road, and the college's many stone buildings add grace to the town. The feeling I had while walking was one of spaciousness. You couldn't help but realize the community had pride in every detail of its appearance.

The white man's settlement in Williamstown began in 1750. The town was first known as West Hoosuck. A blockhouse, stockade and fort were built at the present site of the Williams Inn as a refuge from repeated attacks during the French and Indian Wars. When peace came to the region in 1760, settlers arrived in droves, clearing the woods for agricultural use. Today, many of the farms are reverting back to forest, but the country feeling has not left.

After exploring the town's center we went to the renowned **Sterling and Francine Clark Art Institute**. This houses one of the largest collections of Renoir works in the world. I had my doubts about taking a seven-year-old to an art gallery, but Kristin surprised me with her interest. We made the visit more fun by keeping a list of our favorite paintings, then voting for the winner at the end of the tour. We also kept the visit short. My knowledge of French impressionist painters is little more than Kristin's, but you don't need knowledge to feel moved by beauty. Besides the paintings by Renoir and other masters, I was taken with the works of American artists such as Homer, Sargent and Remington.

We left man's creations of beauty to visit nature's, driving next to **Field Farm**, owned by the Trustees of Reservations. This 294-acre country estate lies at the foot of the Taconic Range and is home to wild turkey, coyote, bear, deer and fox. Osprey, wood ducks, kingfishers and herons visit the pond and marshes. There is even a bed and breakfast in a large home here that offers sweeping views of the fields, forest and Mount Greylock.

Back in Williamstown we took another short walk, this time along the banks of the Hoosic. Just beyond Williams College is an access road to ball fields. This in turn leads to a wonderful river walk that begins near Eph's Pond in a flood plain area that is one of the lowest elevations in the Berkshires. The woods here have giant cottonwoods, box elder, and sycamore (identified by the splashes of white on the grey-brown bark). The river ran swiftly, coursing with riffles over small stones. It appeared to be a great place for trout fishing.

That night we stayed at the **Williams Inn**, located adjacent to the common in the center of town. This features 100 guestrooms on three stories, all decorated in Colonial style. The room in which we stayed was quite comfortable. It had a TV, which allowed Kristin to watch her favorite show, *Dr. Quinn, Medicine Woman.*

Not all trips go according to plan, and sometime during the middle of the night, Kristin awoke with a fever. The inn's manager came to the rescue, going out to purchase Tylenol so I could stay with Kristin. Now that's the kind of service that brings customers back.

Williamstown

If You Go:

The Williams Inn	(413) 458-9371
Mount Greylock State Reservation	(413) 499-4262
Clark Art Institute	(413) 458-9545
Field Farm	(413) 458-3144

Supplemental Directions to Hoosic River Trail: Park on Stetson Road across from Eph's Pond, near barrier gate on right. Follow paved lane bordered by light poles to evergreens, and turn right. Follow about 20 feet to trail on left leading into woods. Proceed to river.

Berkshire Backroads

Tyringham, Monterey & New Marlborough

The backroads above **Tyringham** took me up the ridge and past the old Shaker homes, plain yet handsome in their simplicity. It was a beautiful hilltop high above the valley, a place where road names retained their original meaning. Meadow Road wound through a golden hayfield, Forest Road passed dark and mysterious woods, and Tyringham Road went through town.

Now I was on Breakneck Road, dropping down the precipitous slope, the ancient Subaru growling in low gear. Then into green lowlands, over a stream, and through lush pasture, before turning onto a main road (actually named Main Road) toward town.

Ahead sat a structural oddity that made me slam on the brakes. A real honest-to-goodness gingerbread house, or so it seemed. Its roof was full of waves and curves in colored patterns of grey, brown and rust, like a marbled stone one finds in a streambed.

What kind of person builds such a thing, dares to be so different from his or her neighbors? I had to find out. A sign out front said **Tyringham Art Galleries**, so I went inside.

A woman stood behind a small desk in a cavernous gallery with cathedral ceilings. Her name was Ann Marie Davis, and she and her husband Donald owned the gallery. We fell into conversation and I learned that they bought the building in 1947, just after the death of its original owner and designer, Sir Henry Kitson.

Tyringham Art Gallery

It was Donald who first fell in love with the place. With no job at the time and no idea what he was going to do with the mammoth structure, he put their entire savings toward the downpayment and they became the new owners. He was smitten, and reason went out the window. "At the time, I was scared," Ann said with a smile, "but now, looking back, I'm glad he did it. It was hard work, though. Took us five years to renovate the place to the point where we could open it as a gallery."

The roof was fashioned with a rolling effect that recalls the Berkshire hills. English workers were imported for the construction; they labored on this project for more than two years. The roof – which has a thatched look – is made from traditional materials and has an estimated weight of 80 tons.

But the gingerbread house is much more than an amazing architectural feat. Inside is a treasure trove of paintings and other artwork, while out back is a sculpture garden nestled in quiet woods by a tiny pond. Walking through the gallery and on the garden path, one can appreciate the monumental effort that went into creating something different, something special.

The word "Tyringham" has a nice ring to it, and the center of town did not disappoint me. It reminded me of a Vermont village: a low-lying valley of farmland surrounded by green hills. At the center of town I turned off the main road and onto Church Road, which leads to a hillside cemetery behind Union Church. The view was wonderful. A town such as this ranks high on my list, especially when its backside is as good as its front.

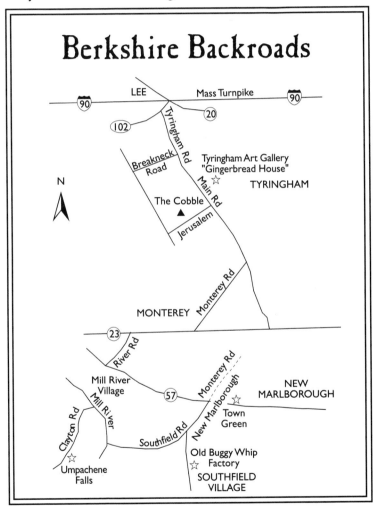

While heading toward the trails at **the Cobble**, I came across four hikers sitting by the side of the road with their gear spread out around them. There were three boys and one girl, all college-age, and all spending the summer hiking the Appalachian Trail (which runs through the Cobble). The foursome had started out at Harpers Ferry, West Virginia about five weeks earlier. They had since covered over 500 miles, with the previous night being one of the roughest yet. They said they could find no water supply and were getting desperate when the sky opened in a downpour. Using ponchos, they were able to funnel rainwater into their cooking pot. It seemed like their troubles were over. But as evening turned to night, thunder and lighting came, whipping the trees above. The group spent some tense moments inside their tents, wondering if a tree would come crashing down upon them in the dark.

However, most of their journey had been filled with pleasant moments. They especially enjoyed meeting friendly people in small towns along the way. "When we go into town," one of them said, "they can smell us coming and know where we've been! Grooming conditions on the trail are not exactly the best. We have had many folks cook us dinners, and have slept in churches, a monastery, private homes, and barns – a nice change from lean-tos."

Wildlife was varied on their trek; they'd spotted a black bear, wild turkey, and even a rattlesnake. "This trip is something we have dreamed of for years, and we plan on going all the way to Mount Katahdin," one of them remarked. All I could say was, "Go for it, before the chains of the working world get you." Such an adventure will provide life-long memories.

And so I left my new friends and ascended the Cobble alone. As I hiked, I imagined this was the start of my journey to Katahdin. What would it be like to be outdoors for weeks, to have no other cares than the path in front of you? Life reduced to its most basic and elemental living. Someday...

The walk up the Cobble is a gentle one, passing through pasture, then woods, and later into a field with goldenrod waving yellow in the breeze. Monarch butterflies floated off in front of me and I felt my spirits soar with them. I was glad I was here alone, free to stop and feel the peace of this place. I lay back, letting my face soak up the September sun.

While in the field I saw two handsome birds. First, a blue bird winged by, and I thought of Thoreau's description, "They carry the sky on their back." Then I spotted a kestrel on a cedar tree. It stayed at the top of the tree, apparently surveying the field for insects or mice. I had a good long look through binoculars at this small falcon, with its rusty back and bluish wings. It is said that kestrels rarely go for larger prey, preferring insects instead. But I once saw one swoop down on a blackbird that was feeding on the ground and kill it in a spray of feathers.

Later I resumed my walk, passing an enchanting stand of white birch and then cresting the summit. Far below, an idyllic Tyringham lay nestled in the valley. When a cloud passed over the sun, it was as though someone had drawn a curtain on the town. Then, just as quickly, the light returned to illuminate the church, the green hills and golden fields. I'm sure there are all types of people living in this valley – both good and bad – but from this vantage point, the town seemed far removed from the troubles that plague the rest of the world.

They say that the Cobble was broken off from nearby Backbone Mountain and flipped over, because the oldest rocks are on the top of the hill. But try as I might, I could not picture the event. The hill seemed too permanent, like God put it here. But perhaps God, like man, changes things after a second look.

The rocks at the Cobble are known as "Tyringham gneiss." Once subjected to great heat and pressure, they have a marbled quality to them, and there are many veins of white quartz mixed with the gneiss. On the trail to the top, you can't miss a tall rock formation standing on its end. This boulder – actually a glacial erratic that was carried here by the ice sheet – seems so out of place that one would think it landed here from outer space.

From the Cobble, I drove south into Monterey, then hit the brakes when I saw **River Road**. A little way down the road was a small waterfall and broad pools. Here, two boys were swinging out over the grey-green water on a rope, and then dropping with a mighty splash. "What the heck?" I thought, putting on a pair of shorts. Shock is probabably not the right word for the feeling that occurred when I hit the water. The cold took most of the air out of my lungs, but I still managed a scream as I motored furiously to shore. Yet, within minutes, I was on the rope again. It was as though years had fallen away; I was 10 years old again, invigorated and totally alive.

River Road led down to **New Marlborough**, where the village green on Route 57 is a classic, complete with an inn. The **Old Inn On The Green** was built in 1760 and was an important resting spot for weary travelers making the overland journey from Westfield to Sheffield. The inn also served as a post office in 1806, with mail arriving once a week by horseback. Later, a stagecoach brought the mail daily on the "Red Bird Line." The latter ran from Albany to Hartford one day, and then reversed direction the next.

The inn and common look much as they did long ago, and a tired traveler can still find lodging and dining in this handsome building. For some, the location may be too quiet and out of the way, but for others, that's the very reason to come. One of the best things about the setting is the old **Monterey-New Marlborough Road,** which begins by the side of the inn and passes northward through woods and fields free of power lines and development. Old stone walls built by settlers more than a century and a half ago still stand firmly along the trail. Farmers built the walls from rocks turned up by the plow, using them to mark their property lines or enclose their herds and flocks. Neighbors helped one another when the job was large. "Stone-bees" were held, with oxen and many strong arms removing the rocks and crafting the walls.

Southfield Road leaves the green and winds toward the **Old Buggy Whip Factory,** which now houses antique dealers, craft shops and a café. At the nearby village of **Mill River,** I stopped at the old general store and struck up a conversation with the owner. I remarked how this is my kind of country. He responded by saying, "Yes, it's the last place." He meant that this was one region yet to be developed on a large scale. It really was one of the last *best* places. To underscore what he said, I went down to **Umpachene Falls,** where two rivers converge. One of the rivers cascades down a series of ledges before mingling with the other river. A kingfisher, with its distinctive crested head, flew over the river with irregular wingbeats. Aside from the bird, I had the place to myself.

The falls are named after a Mahican Indian sachem, and surely Native Americans would have had a village or a camp here. The location would have provided both drinking water and fishing. Indeed, the spot where the rivers join would have been deep enough to float the dugout canoes used by tribes in southern New England. I wondered if these Indians could possibly have foreseen that this would be the "last best place?"

If You Go:

Tyringham Art Galleries	(413) 243-3260
The Old Inn On The Green	(413) 229-3131

Along the Housatonic

Stockbridge, Great Barrington, Egremont, Mount Washington & Ashley Falls

"What an appealing start to a walk," I thought, surveying the narrow footbridge over the **Housatonic**. With no traffic to worry about on the other side of the river, off I went over the bridge, then up the trail into the Ice Glen.

The ravine known as the **Ice Glen** was named for the cool mini-climate within this boulder-filled chasm. Even in late spring, the air is dank and cold, and deposits of ice still linger. Little sunlight enters the bottom of the ravine, and its narrowness and depth help keep temperatures from rising. Above the ravine is a trail that leads to **Laura's Lookout**, offering exceptional views of Stockbridge and the surrounding countryside. The trail that leads to this hilltop is reached by going left at the fork in the path, just minutes after crossing the suspension bridge. It's only about three-quarters of a mile to the top and the ascent is gradual.)

As remarkable as the geology of the Ice Glen is, the real reason I came was for the trees. Bob Leverett, an expert on old-growth forests, first told me about this wonderful place. He described magnificent white pines and hemlocks that have grown here for centuries. Large trees have always fascinated me, and I share Robert Frost's sentiments when he wrote, "If I tire of trees, I seek again mankind."

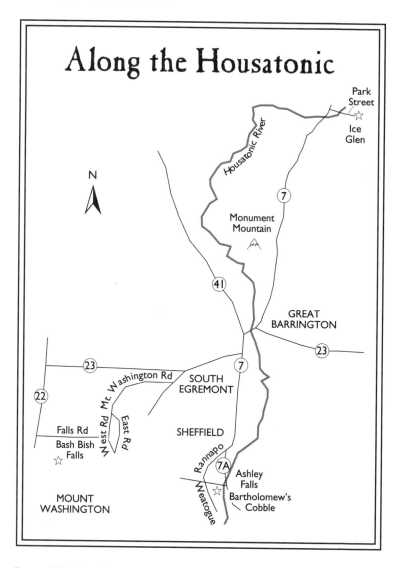

Along the Housatonic

It would be hard to tire of the trees at the Ice Glen. Some are so large that when you look up, they seem to touch the clouds (making you dizzy in the process). The combination of grand old trees and sheer silence gives the place a mystical, cathedral-like quality.

I was so taken with the giant pines that I wrote to Leverett for more information. He told me that the Ice Glen stand includes two incredibly tall pine trees that are over 140 feet in height, with girths of nine feet. Their age is estimated at 100-150 years. In addition, there is also an old-growth section of trees 300 years old. One exceeds 12 feet in circumference and is 134 feet high. There is also a stand of native red pines. A rare treat indeed and, at 200 years old, probably the oldest in the state.

To fully appreciate the need to preserve the old-growth forest, one must look at man's impact on New England's landscape over the past 400 years. When the first Europeans arrived in the New World, only a tiny portion of land had been cleared by the native Algonkin Indian tribes. Miles and miles of virgin forest served as a home to wolves, bears, and even mountain lions. However, in his quest for more agricultural land and lumber, the white man quickly changed the face of New England. By 1900, 75-85% of southern New England was either field or pasture. And in northern New England, almost every acre had been logged. In his beautifully written *Guide to New England's Landscape*, Neil Jorgensen wrote, "In the 19th century, naturalists were warning New Englanders that fearful consequences would ensue if the countryside became disrobed of trees." That gives us some indication of just how devoid of trees the region was at that time.

Today, much of the land has returned to forest as farmland has been abandoned. But most of the more visible woodlands are comprised of trees under 100 years old. The few remaining old-growth tracts are located in hilly regions that were too steep for 19th-century logging techniques.

Finding a patch of forest that has never been disturbed takes the patience, know-how, and physical endurance of men like Leverett. He explained that 400 years seems to be the maximum age a tree can live in this region, although he still has hopes of finding a 500-year-old specimen. Besides counting the rings on downed trees, Leverett looks for other clues: no sign of human disturbance, a thriving community of shade-tolerant ferns and herbaceous plants on the forest floor, and seedlings on the ground that are the same species as the adults.

The eastern old-growth tracts do not have the stunning proportions of the Pacific Northwest forests, and it takes a trained eye to spot our remaining patches of ancient woodlands. Leverett's son Bob Jr., who works with his father in searching and cataloguing the virgin stands, said, "The old-growth forest canopy has an unmistakable look – even from three or four miles away."

Another reason I love this region is that there is one fascinating place to explore after another, some within a stone's throw of each other. **Monument Mountain**, rising 1,700 feet above sea level, is just south of the Ice Glen on Route 7. It has spectactular views, a number of hiking trails, and a rich diversity of flora and fauna. On my visit, I took a moment at the base of the mountain to study the trail signs. On the left was the "easy" trail, and on the right, the "steep" trail. I went right, ignoring the fact that my belt was on its last notch. (The minute you start taking the easy way, the battle of the waistline is lost – or so my theory goes.) The start of the trail was deceptively flat, passing beneath a canopy of maple, ash and beech.

But soon the trail became steeper, and boulders made the footing more difficult. In no time, I was winded. I sat in the shade of some old maples to catch my breath. A couple of hikers passed me – which I didn't mind – but then came a man carrying a two-year-old in a "baby pack." That got me back on my feet. Within half an hour I was on the ridge, where stunted pine, mountain laurel and white birch grew in the sun. I was greeted by a 360° view; the open summit looked like a wonderful place to picnic. That's exactly what Herman Melville, Oliver Wendell Holmes and Nathaniel Hawthorne did when they climbed to the peak in 1850. From that very first meeting, Hawthorne and Melville were life-long friends. (Later, Melville even dedicated *Moby Dick* to Hawthorne.)

I, too, made friends at the top – a couple who lived nearby. We discussed the differences between western and eastern Massachusetts. I've lived half my life in each part of the state and have observed that while many easterners dream of going west, no one from the Berkshires wants to go east. Residents of western Massachusetts think that the politicians in Boston ignore their part of the state, and many distrust the government. Who can blame them – just read the history of Shays' Rebellion, or the seizure of the Swift River Valley to create Quabbin Reservoir.

One of my favorite villages, **South Egremont**, is located just south of Monument Mountain on Route 41. The entire downtown area is a National Historic District. The **Gaslight Store** will make you feel as though you stepped back into the last century, and you can still purchase penny candy for a penny. Nearby is **Mom's Country Café**, where breakfast is served all day.

My daughter Kristin and I once spent a wonderful father/daughter weekend at the **Weathervane Inn** in South Egremont. It was a charming place, an elegant farm and coach house situated on 10 acres of land. Thinking back, I remember how much closer that trip brought the two of us – perhaps the adventure of the journey allowed me to see the child in a new light. On that trip, Kristin seemed almost grown up, a real traveling companion. She responded by treating me as both father and friend.

One of the places we explored was **Bash Bish Falls**, just down the road in Mount Washington. I've been told the easiest way to reach the falls is via Copake, New York, but we felt adventurous and took the rutted backroads through Mount Washington. I'm glad we did. On the way, five deer bounded out across the road, "flags" waving, and down a steep hillside. One seemed to literally sail over a cliff in the most graceful leap imaginable. Nearby, at a turn in the road, we walked to a rock promenade that offered a spectacular view west to New York.

The falls are probably the most impressive in the Bay State. They drop 200 feet in a series of cascades through granite outcroppings, with the final 80-foot drop divided into two cataracts. There is a trail leading to the top of the falls, where the sound of rushing water combined with the extreme height makes for an exciting walk.

Timber rattlers still inhabit this remote section of the state. They can sometimes be seen sunning themselves in the gorge. Once back on the road, be sure to follow Route 7 south into Sheffield. On the right side are three homes tightly clustered together. These date to the 18th and 19th centuries and one now houses the town's historic society. In the morning, the sun strikes these handsome structures, making for a wonderful picture.

At Ashley Falls there is a great view of the Housatonic at **Bartholomew's Cobble**. The Mahican Indians gave the river its name – which means "place beyond the mountains"– while the early settlers called it "Great River." In his book, The Housatonic, Chard Power Smith wrote, "In volume it is of the second order, smaller than the Connecticut 40 miles to the east, or the Hudson 40 miles to the west. Yet it is large enough to suggest the power and majesty of the cosmos, and the first colonists of its banks, men who had seen bigger streams, called it the Great River."

There are numerous bends and marshes on this river, which serves as a migratory stopover for many birds and ducks. Indeed, the Housatonic is said to be one of the most biologically diverse rivers in the state because of the abundant marble and limestone outcrops that neutralize the acidity of the soil over which it flows. This marble – which dates back 500 million years – can be seen at

Bartholomew's Cobble. Many rare and unusual lime-loving plants can also be found here. In April, the flowers of the round-leaved hepatica plant show a range of hues, from pure white to deep cobalt. Along with the hepatica, there are over 450 other species of wildflowers growing here.

One could spend a whole day at the Cobble, first visiting the small natural history museum, then walking the riverside trails. Serious walkers should cross Weatogue Road and follow the paths that pass meadows and head northward to the historic **Colonel John Ashley House**. Built in 1735, the Colonel Ashley House contains furniture and household objects from the 18th and early 19th centuries. Besides being the oldest dwelling in Berkshire County, it was also the site of the Sheffield Declaration, a petition against British tyranny, written in 1773.

Housatonic River by Bartholemew's Cobble

If You Go:

Colonel John Ashley House
   & Bartholomew's Cobble   (413) 229-8600
Weathervane Inn   (413) 528-9580

Central Hill Towns

Chesterfield, Worthington, Middlefield, & Chester

I love traveling with a river by my side, so I turned off Route 143 and followed the **Westfield River** southward. Just beyond the crossroads at the village of Chesterfield is a canyon carved by the rushing waters of Westfield River's west branch at **Chesterfield Gorge**. Towering above the river are sheer granite cliffs; down below are smooth, water-worn rock formations that look something like waves. The waters pound through the narrow passage in spring, while the summertime low water is a picture of tranquility.

At the upper end of the gorge is the stone foundation of **High Bridge**, which dates to 1739. The bridge was once part of the Boston to Albany Post Road. In the Trustees of Reservations' brochure, I read that, during the Revolutionary War, the Redcoats marched over this bridge heading toward Boston and their ships after being defeated at Saratoga. Try as I might, I simply cannot visualize an army of Redcoats marching through this quiet, forested spot.

After stopping at the **Knightsville Dam** – where the broad flood plain was shrouded in mist – I went on to Worthington. For me, the rain was a nuisance. But inside the Corners Grocery I heard a very different perspective. A woman with a big smile on her face raised both arms to the sky and said, "Ah, sweet rain, I can almost see the corn dancing." If you make your livelihood off the land, sudden showers can be quite welcome.

Worthington is a good place to visit, no matter the season. Winter brings cross-country skiers to **Hickory Hill Ski Touring Center**, while early spring is maple sugar time. Summer is the best season for both hiking and fishing, and fall is perfect for cruising back-roads and soaking up the wonderful foliage. When we think of autumn's colors, many of us think of Vermont and New Hampshire. But the Berkshires are equally impressive. The country roads that wind through Worthington are lined by giant sugar maples that can turn a whole hillside bright yellow and orange come October. There are some particularly impressive maples along Route 143 near the Worthington Inn, a handsome colonial farmhouse dating back to 1780. The inn has three guestrooms, five fireplaces and is filled with period antiques. Across the way is a large field where horses graze behind the stone wall.

Corners Grocery, Worthington

From Worthington, **Glendale Falls** is only about five miles as the crow flies. Because of the large tract of forest along the middle branch of the Westfield River, the drive there is more than twice as long. But if you're in the area and you love waterfalls as I do, you won't want to miss it. Cascading 150 feet over rock ledges, Glendale Brook tumbles toward the river valley below. A small footpath follows the brook down the hill, offering a variety of interesting photographic opportunities. I'm partial to the picture at the very top of the falls looking downstream, where the brook suddenly drops from sight.

Surrounding the falls is a forest of hemlock and beech, with an understory of mountain laurel. The serenity there was wonderful. It's easy to take silence for granted, but think how rare it's becoming. Seems there is always noise – cars, TV, radio, even the annoying beep of E-mail on your computer. But, as I walked the woods at Glendale Falls, the only sounds were an occasional bird song and the muted splashing of the brook in the distance. Thank God for quiet places.

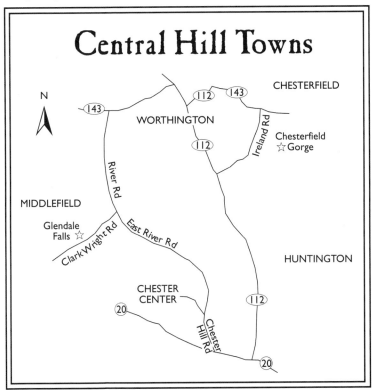

Later, with maps spread before me in the parking area of Glendale Falls, I noticed that River Road hugged the middle branch of the Westfield River for a good distance. I decided to take that road, and worry about where it led later.

It was a beautiful drive, an isolated stretch of asphalt with plenty of spots along the river where you could stop to read, write, or just cool your feet. I tried to do all three, but the lure of the trout was too much.

Donning an old pair of sneakers, I walked up the river. The summer's drought made walking easy but catching trout difficult. There was, however, one advantage to low water: when I cast my fly into a tree on the opposite bank, it was relatively easy to wade across and retrieve it. Not the sort of thing to brag about but, if you're in the habit of losing flies, it's nice to be able to save one now and then.

It was hot, so I found a pool deep enough to sit in. With my clothes on the bank, I took special care to place my glasses squarely on top of them. It was only a couple of months earlier that I had a bad experience doing precisely the same thing. At that time, I'd walked a couple miles through the woods, blazing my own trail to reach a river (visions of giant trout make us do crazy things). Later, I went for a swim in the river and when I came out I couldn't find my glasses. Now, only those who wear glasses can understand the panic that swept through me. The thought of trying to negotiate my way out of dense woods with blurry vision was not a prospect I relished. There was a real chance of getting lost or injuring myself. I searched everywhere for the glasses, believing I had placed them atop my clothes. I don't know what I would have done if the sun had not reflected off the metal frames, because the glasses were not on my clothes but on a rock a few feet away in the river. To this day I don't remember putting them there, but I do recall the relief of being able to see again.

This time, the glasses were right where I left them. I let the sun dry me off, then found my way back to the car and headed south. The trip was somewhat unusual because I had no real destination in mind. I'd let the road and curiosity be my guide. In his book, *Blue Highways*, William Least Heat Moon used the same approach to exploration. He wrote, "Had I gone looking for some particular place, rather than any place, I never would have found this spring under the sycamores."

On my map I saw **Chester Center**. The word "center" often means the old part of town, and this was no exception. An old church, even older homes, and a graveyard were all that made up this forgotten and peaceful place.

Later, on Route 8, I chuckled when I saw one of those "Adopt a Highway" signs emblazoned with the name of a Boy Scout troop. Looked to me like the state had gotten the Boy Scouts to become "litter-picker-uppers." Let's hope the Scouts still learn a little woodcraft, like making a fire in the rain.

If You Go:

Worthington Inn   (413) 238-4441

Chesterfield Gorge is located on River Road in West Chesterfield; swimming is not allowed. For information, call (413) 684-0148.

Glendale Falls is on Clark Wright Road in Middlefield. Call (413) 298-3239.

Along the Great River

The Connecticut River & Pioneer Valley: Holyoke, South Hadley, Hadley, South Deerfield & Northfield

Like two sentinels guarding the rich lowlands below, Mount Sugarloaf and Mount Holyoke tower above the **Pioneer Valley**. The mountains are not particularly high, but because they rise so abruptly from the flat flood plains along the Connecticut River, the views are spectacular. The scene is especially beautiful in autumn, when the hills are cloaked in a blaze of color. Surely this is the way all visitors should first see the Pioneer Valley. The vista is much the way the valley would have looked hundreds of years ago when it was considered New England's breadbasket. Back then, thousands of bushels of wheat were shipped from this fertile land to coastal towns such Boston, Plymouth and Providence.

On my last visit to the area, I started my exploration at **Mount Holyoke** and then followed the river northward to Mount Sugarloaf, with many stops in between. One of the nice things about Mount Holyoke is that you don't have to have the strength of a mountain goat to reach its summit; you can drive right to the top from an entrance off Route 47 in Hadley. Of course, if you like a challenge, there are miles of hiking trails here – all part of the 390-acre **Skinner State Park**.

From the summit you will see a checkerboard of green, brown and golden fields below. Winding through the middle is a ribbon of blue – the mighty **Connecticut River**, which originates at the Canadian border and flows approximately 400 miles south to Long Island Sound. In the distance, reddish-orange mountains frame this bucolic scene. September and October is also a good time for hawk watching, as the raptors ride the thermals in their southerly migration. Thermals – the rising columns of hot air created by the combination of valley, mountains, and weather conditions – attract the hawks. Rather than continuously flapping their wings, they can soar in these columns of air, sometimes grouping together to form "kettles."

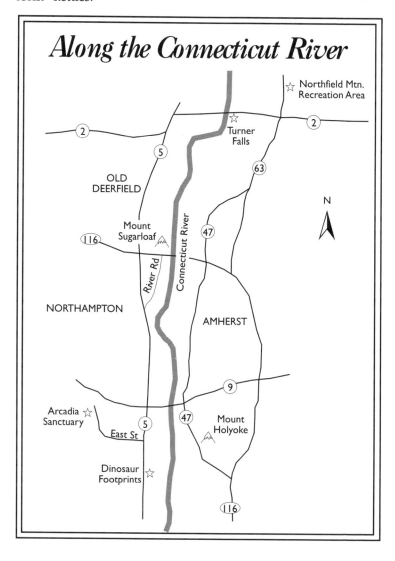

Mount Holyoke is part of the east-west chain of mountains called the **Holyoke Range**. This orientation is unique since all the other hills in the region run north-south, including the Berkshires. Another unusual feature seen from the summit is the "oxbow," the old U-shaped channel of the river that lies in Northampton. In 1840 an ice jam caused the river to change course, shortening it by 3½ miles. In the process, Hadley lost 400 acres to Northampton – imagine the lawsuits if that happened today!

Besides the natural marvels seen from Mount Holyoke, you can enjoy one of man's better efforts in **The Prospect House**, a mountain-top inn built in the early 1800s. Even though the building no longer serves its original purpose, you can sit in the shade of its porch and watch the broad-winged hawks sail by. When The Prospect House was first built, guests were brought up the mountain on a tramway. This was first powered by horses, then steam, and, later, electricity. What a grand place it must have been, and what a grand view to wake up to! Up to 300 citizens of Northampton and Hadley began work on The Prospect House in 1821, carrying all the supplies up the mountain. Fueled by "a little water with a good deal of brandy in it," the original structure was quickly completed, measuring 15 by 22 feet. Later expansion allowed the tramway to carry over 100,000 tourists a year to the summit. Hilltops were popular picnicking spots in the 19th century. Even today, experienced travelers know the joys of spreading out a blanket and dining among the clouds.

Not far from Mount Holyoke is something far older than The Prospect House; older, in fact, than mankind. Set in rock are a number of clear depressions made by dinosaurs. The prints are about 15 inches long and show the three toes of Eubrontes, a 20-foot carnivore that once roamed New England. At that time – approximately 200 million years ago – this region was far different than it is today. Giant ferns and palm-like pines grew in a much warmer climate. This place may not match the drama of *Jurassic Park*, but standing in the exact spot where a dinosaur once lumbered is fascinating in its own way.

The tracks can be found at **Dinosaur Footprints Reservation**, a small eight-acre property in Holyoke owned by the Trustees of Reservations. Although the reservation is adjacent to Route 5 on the west bank of the Connecticut River, it is not well-marked and is therefore easy to miss. Going north on Route 91, take Exit 17A (Route 141 East to Holyoke) and turn north on Route 5 for 2.2 miles until you see an unmarked turnoff on the right.

Nearby, on the border of Easthampton and Northampton, is **Arcadia Wildlife Sanctuary**. These 530 acres of woods, fields and marsh in the flood plain of the Connecticut River Valley offer some of the region's best birding. The sanctuary also abuts part of the aforementioned oxbow; this is, in fact, the subject of a wonderful painting by Thomas Cole. Many people think that the river continues to flow through the oxbow, but this wide semi-circle of water is actually a lake. Over time it will fill in, as the surrounding vegetation inches closer.

Arcadia has an observation tower that rises above a marsh. Here, with the aid of binoculars, you can spot great blue herons, wood ducks, muskrats, and maybe even a deer. There are signs on the tower that mark the high water level of floods in 1936 and 1984. They serve as reminders that lowlands like these are occasionally overtaken by rising water. Man is slowly learning that the best flood control plan is to leave nature's own marshes and flood plains untouched. They can then act as giant sponges, allowing spring run-off to fan out and be released into the river gradually.

From Arcadia Wildlife Sanctuary, you can set out to explore some of the nearby areas. The towns on the east side of the river are especially good to get lost in. **Pelham, Hadley** and **Granby** all have a quiet, rural character, along with some "characters" who are not so quiet. I recall hiking up a stream in Pelham when I heard loud singing up ahead. Rounding a bend, I came across an older gentleman standing buck-naked beneath a waterfall. I gave him a wide berth, wondering if he were sane. Later, as I retraced my steps along the stream, I saw that the man had gone. Hot and sweaty, I stripped, waded in, and let the cool water invigorate me. Then I, too, began to sing a little song...

If you prefer to stay closer to the river, try following **River Road**, which begins in Hatfield and follows the Connecticut northward all the way to South Deerfield. Fields of pumpkin, peppers, tomatoes, onions, and corn lie between the road and the river. Barns and tobacco sheds dot the landscape.

I love the view of **Mount Sugarloaf** from River Road in Whately. It seems to rise out of nowhere, blocking the road ahead. You can drive right to the top, as you can at Mount Holyoke, for another spectacular view. The white steepled church in Sunderland makes the vista a perfect New England scene; photographers love this shot. Below, the Connecticut River flows straight, looking more

like a canal than the meandering waterway seen from Mount
Holyoke.

The best way to fully appreciate the diversity of the Connecticut
River is on a river cruise. One is available on the **Quinnetuket II.**
(Quinnetuket is the Indian name for this body of water; it translates
to "long tidal river.") An open-air boat with canopy and benches,
the *Quinnetuket II* leaves from Northfield Mountain Recreation and
Environmental Center in Northfield, and travels 12 miles down-
river. The outings are made all the more interesting by knowledgeable guides who discuss the river's history and its natural lore.

French King Bridge

Early in the cruise the boat passes beneath the **French King Bridge**,
which spans the river between Erving and Gill. Completed in 1932,
this bridge won a national prize as the most beautiful steel bridge
in its class. Rising 140 feet above the river and stretching 700 feet,
it took just six months to build at a cost of $375,000. (The bridge's
arch was something of a magnet for daredevil pilots who would
illegally fly their plane beneath it!)

Here, the banks are steep-sided and covered with pine, hemlock,
oak and maple. We saw hawks and herons, but never caught sight

of the bald eagles that now nest along the river. The eagles are one of the state's environmental success stories, having expanded from their original introduction at Quabbin Reservoir to sites such as Barton's Cove on the Connecticut River. These majestic birds pair for life and will return to the same nest for years. They feed primarily on fish during the warm weather months, supplementing their winter diet with meat from deer or other animals that die during winter.

The river sustains not only wildlife, but mankind, offering an inexpensive source of hydroelectric power. In the not-too-distant past, the river also was a means of transportation for the logging industry. Log drives in the last century took advantage of the river's current as timber was floated out of the north woods in the spring and ended up at the mills in Massachusetts and Connecticut by summer. If ever there was a dangerous job, it was that of the river man. It was up to him to keep the logs moving, either by stringing cables from them to oxen on shore, or by walking out on the logs and freeing them with poles. If those methods didn't break up the logjams, dynamite was used.

While on the boat, I couldn't help but wish I had X-ray vision. This would enable me to see into the water and discover what types of fish were beneath me. Afterwards, I found a way to do just that – by visiting the fishway at **Turners Falls**. It is a wondrous thing to see first-hand the underwater journey of fish completing their natural cycle of life. In the spring, migrating shad can be seen through glass windows looking into the fishway. Here, they fight the current in their annual run upstream. Shad are members of the herring family. They are anadromous fish that spend most of their life in salt water and return to fresh water to spawn. Before the construction of dams, it is estimated that the shad run on the Connecticut River was as high as six million fish annually.

Two huge lamprey eels also came through the ladder while I was there. Outfitted with cylinder-shaped mouths resembling suction cups, they attached themselves to the glass and rested. An ugly fish, to be sure, but in the river, looks don't count. The eels, in fact, had a heart-warming effect on me, taking me back in time. For a moment, I was a nine-year-old boy again, wandering the banks of the "Long Tidal River" near my home in Longmeadow. I recalled being mesmerized by the lamprey that swam up Longmeadow Brook. Whether you're on a boat, walking the shore, or looking into a fish ladder, a river has the power to move you. Go see for yourself!

If You Go:

The *Quinnetuket II* operates from the end of May through mid-October. Reservations are required. Call (413) 659-3714.

Turners Falls Fishways/Fishladders: Viewing starts in May for the fish run. Located on 1st Street, off Avenue A in Turners Falls. (There is also a viewing center at the Holyoke Fishladder.) For visiting hours at both locations, call (413) 659-3714.

Arcadia Wildlife Sanctuary is on Combs Road in Easthampton. Call (413) 584-3009.

Mount Holyoke is part of Skinner State Park, a 390-acre park located along Route 47 in Hadley. The road leading to the summit is open from April through November, while the hiking trails can be used year-round.

The Prospect House (now called the Summit House) is open on weekends from May to October; it offers historical displays and special events.

For information on **Skinner State Park** and all it contains, call (413) 586-0350.

Dinosaur Footprints Reservation is owned by The Trustees of Reservations and is located at a small unmarked turnoff on Route 5, about 5.2 miles south from Exit 18 off Interstate 91.

Central Massachusetts

A Slice of
Old New England

Belchertown, Pelham, & New Salem

Situated along the western shore of massive Quabbin Reservoir, the village of **New Salem** just might be the most charming in all the Bay State. The town's center looks like a place that time forgot, with the character of the region well-preserved.

One of the reasons that New Salem has managed to protect its beauty is that **Quabbin Reservoir** hugs its eastern border, guaranteeing that no development will encroach upon the town's center. In fact, the road that leads past the village green abruptly ends when it reaches the watershed's forest. That makes this the only town center I know that is not located at a crossroads. Instead, it's just a spot of utter peace.

Because the town road leads "nowhere," few people have ever seen New Salem's charming center. I recall the weekend I inadvertantly wandered into town, thinking I had finally found the slice of Old New England for which I'd been searching. It was winter, and the bare trees starkly contrasted with the simple white homes that ringed the common. A granite bench and ancient hitching post gave the feeling that this town had never emerged from the prior century. Best of all were the twin white church steeples that thrust heavenwards through a crystal blue sky. Needless to say, I took one photograph after another.

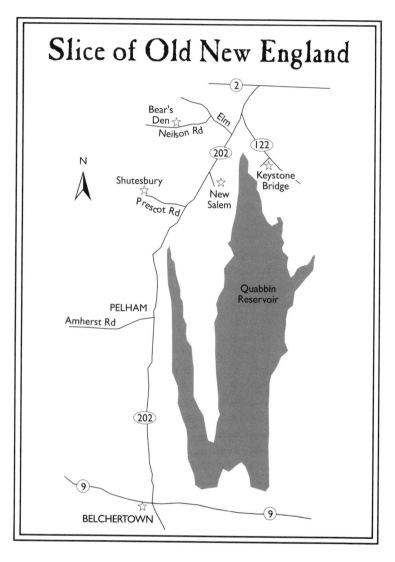

Slice of Old New England

Behind the fire station and ball field, I followed a trail through woods of maple and hemlock to an overlook above Quabbin Reservoir. The snow crunched underfoot, but the woods were still; not even a blue jay or a crow called out. I was surprised that my footsteps were the first sign of human activity to break the two-day-old crust of snow. Didn't anyone else see the beauty in our frozen white landscape? Perhaps the lure of Sunday afternoon football is greater than the call of the wild, turning us into a nation of spectators rather than participants. Well, I guess I shouldn't complain. After all, I had the woods to myself.

Back in town, I wondered if the common had at one time contained stocks. In bygone days, these were used as a means of public humiliation. I could almost picture a poor soul sitting with feet and arms locked in the wooden structure for hours. Besides the usual crimes of drunkenness and blasphemy, people could be punished for idleness or wearing certain clothing and hats considered too fancy. The first stocks used in the colonies were erected by a builder named Edward Palmer, who was hired by the general court in 1640. One of the stocks' original purposes was to punish those who charged prices deemed too high for their goods or services. In one of life's true ironies, Palmer finished building the stocks and presented his bill, only to have the court pronounce it excessive. As a result, Palmer became the first American put into the stocks.

New Salem Village Green

New Salem Center may not have had stocks, but today they have something much more useful in man's quest for self-improvement: **The Common Reader Bookshop**. It was closed on my first visit, but I've since returned and enjoyed browsing through a wide assortment of old and used books. When I'm in a shop like this, I like to look for books about the area I'm exploring. Here, I learned that in the 1930s, the construction of a new reservoir meant that

7,500 bodies buried in the cemeteries of the four towns to be flooded (Dana, Enfield, Prescott and Greenwich) had to be reinterred in Ware's Quabbin Park Cemetery. When Boston needed water, not even the dead could rest in peace.

As I walked the perimeter of the green, I wondered why it had taken me so long to find this beautiful place. Was it because I had ignored my home state during my younger years, searching instead for more distant horizons? The words of Raymond Baker (pen name: David Grayson), an earlier writer who lived in Amherst, floated into my consciousness: "Is it not marvelous how far afield some of us are willing to travel in pursuit of that beauty which we leave behind at home? We mistake unfamiliarity for beauty."

To wander the backroads of New Salem is pure pleasure; a chance to see the things that make New England special. **Bullard Farm Bed and Breakfast** is one of those places. This 1793 farm house is one of the few bed and breakfasts that has stayed "in the family." The inn is owned and operated by Janet Kraft, a direct descendent of the Bullard Brothers, a prominent 18th-century lumber family.

I love the place because of the building's character, the owner's hospitality, and the natural setting. Here, you can take a brisk walk through a forest of hemlocks and mountain laurels along the banks of the middle branch of the Swift River. You might notice signs of the mills that once operated here. While I wandered through these woods, I saw signs of deer, porcupine, and fox – all of which had used the same trail.

Strolling through the farm's property, I realized I had acquired a new wisdom: sometimes paradise is right under your feet.

Near Bullard Farm on Neilson Road is the **Bear's Den**, a scenic waterfall with its own historic past. Legend has it that King Philip, the Wampanoag leader of the first wide-scale Indian uprising, held a victory celebration here after attacking towns in the Pioneer Valley. The war was waged because the Indians felt the white men were taking advantage of them.

The waterfall here is quite beautiful. Amidst the shade of giant pines and hemlocks, the stream cascades in a spray of white, its fall split by a large rock before it reaches the grey-green waters of the pool below. Incidentally, Bear's Den was named by a settler who killed a black bear here many years ago.

Today there are fewer bears, but their numbers are on the rise again. I wonder when I will see my first one in Massachusetts. Having met one on a hiking trail in Vermont, it's an experience I would love to repeat – as long as it's in the daytime.

As forests replace farmland, bears, coyotes, and even moose are returning to the Bay State – and maybe, just maybe, mountain lions will too. I've met a couple of very knowledgeable woodsmen who swear they have seen a cougar at Quabbin. Paul Rezendes, author of *Tracking and Art of Seeing*, has never seen a mountain lion here. But he thinks there is a cougar (or cougars) roaming the forests of Quabbin and the Berkshires. "The question," he said, "is not whether there is a cougar living in the wild, but whether or not there is a breeding population." Rezendes believes that a couple of mountain lions were illegally released from captivity and have adapted to the wild. Another theory is that mountain lions living in New Brunswick have moved south into New England.

The middle branch of the Swift, located just to the north, also has its own unique history and wildlife. Spanning the river is the **Keystone Bridge**, a beautiful arched structure constructed of closely fitted stone blocks. Built in the late 1800s, it now serves as a reminder that this was a peaceful valley of mills and farms long before the reservoir. The bridge can be found by walking a few feet down Gate 30, within the boundaries of Quabbin Reservoir.

I once spent an afternoon following the middle branch of the **Swift River** downstream to the point where its waters spill into the northernmost tip of the Quabbin. I saw partridges, two deer and signs of beaver. Like the mountain lion, the beaver was virtually gone from Massachusetts by the year 1800. Loss of habitat and heavy trapping during the 18th century depleted their numbers throughout the northeast, almost to the point of extinction. The fact that beavers are thriving here again is an environmental success story. Much of the credit for this achievement to the Division of Fisheries and Wildlife.

Beavers returned to the state by entering the West Stockbridge area from New York in 1928. State biologist Tom Decker says that the Division of Fisheries and Wildlife assisted in their re-establishment beginning in the 1940s by trapping and transplanting beaver from complaint sites to more suitable habitats. They are now well established in western and central Massachusetts, pushing eastward into the Sudbury River Valley.

In the forests surrounding Quabbin Reservoir, there are signs of these large rodents on almost every stream. Dams are constructed of brush, sticks and saplings, plastered together with mud and vegetation. Dome-shaped lodges are made from the same material. Each lodge contains a sleeping chamber above the water line, with at least two different points of entry or underwater escapes. In the winter, vapor from the inside of the lodge can sometimes be seen rising from its top.

While the beavers can be a nuisance – their activities are known to trigger flooding on roadways and other property – they can also have a positive environmental impact. The ponds they create serve as excellent habitats for waterfowl and other species of wildlife. For example, the standing timber in these ponds can be used by wood ducks (who build their nests inside tree cavities) or by great blue herons (who construct nests at the top of the largest flooded trees). The wetlands are also important in flood control, pollution control, and ground water recharge.

Beavers have dammed a brook by Route 2 in Littleton, and the resulting pond has attracted great blue herons to the timber. Usually, great blue heron colonies are located deep within a swamp, inaccessible to humans. But this colony is just 50 feet from the highway. Not surprisingly, curious motorists often pull over to gawk at the massive birds with their six-foot wing spans. The herons may get all the attention, but it's the beavers who did the work.

It's theorized that a beaver slaps its tail on the water either to warn other beavers of danger or to scare away intruders. It certainly scared me once. I was fishing with three college friends at a pond one night, enjoying good conversation and the quiet of the woods, when the water appeared to explode in front of us. Like true woodsmen, we dropped our poles and ran – that's how loud the slap sounded.

More recently, I was floating on an inner tube at the pond by my Vermont cabin, just staring upward and watching the clouds sail by the treetops. Nothing could be more relaxing – until I had the life scared out of me by a beaver who swam behind me and whacked its tail just four feet from my ear. I fell out of the inner tube, surfacing just in time to see the beaver stare at me, then swim away.

New Salem is not the only town on the west side of Quabbin that has benefited from having Quabbin as a neighbor. Shutesbury, Pelham and Belchertown all have very pleasant town centers and limited traffic.

Shutesbury Center is on a hilltop with an old church, a town hall, and a little red library, while Pelham's is located right next to Route 202. Pelham's town hall is said to be the oldest in continual use throughout New England and is listed on the National Register of Historic Places. This was the home of Daniel Shays, who is best remembered as the leader of Shays' Rebellion (1787). He encouraged farmers in the central and western parts of the state to revolt against the taxes imposed on them by the political powers in Boston. Like King Philip's War and the uprising of the Indians, violence tends to erupt when people feel their voices are going unheard.

Belchertown – the butt of many jokes because of its name – has a town center that is the envy of most communities. A long common is surrounded by shops, old homes, and tall maples. An unusually tall bandstand dominates the green. The annual fair is held here in September. It's a chance to see the town at its best.

The waters that swallowed the towns of Dana, Greenwich, Prescott, and Enfield now lap gently on the shores of the surviving towns. Four towns lost, four towns saved.

If You Go:

Bullard Farm Bed & Breakfast   (508) 544-6959
Common Reader Bookshop   (508) 544-7039

The Hills of South-Central Massachusetts

Sturbridge, Brookfield, West Brookfield, Hardwick, Barre & Petersham

Strange two-foot spires of ice rose from the floor of the tunnel, causing me to creep forward for a better look. Why were there no icicles hanging from the roof, I asked myself, and how did these stalagmites of clear ice defy gravity by "growing" to such large proportions? Perhaps it was so cold that water dripping from the cave's ceiling froze where it landed, each drop adding to the formation. Still, that didn't explain why there were no conventional icicles. I turned away from the little cave, not knowing the answer but glad to have seen such beauty on a frozen winter's day.

I was exploring the forest of **Tantiusques Reservation** in Sturbridge, hoping to ease my cabin fever by embracing the winter world rather than fleeing from it. The tunnel I had seen was created by local miners who once worked this vein of soft black graphite sandwiched between the granite hills. One normally associates mining with the Rockies, and this was the first cave I had come across in Massachusetts.

The trails through Tantiusques were dazzling in the winter light, with white snow covering the forest floor and mountain laurel sparkling in the sun. Deer tracks were everywhere, but the woods were as still as could be. Not even the usual calls of blue jays or crows broke the spell. My cabin fever was fading away; the simple act of walking was working its magic.

I reached the end of the trail more quickly than I'd expected, but then looked at my watch and realized an hour had passed. Like any activity that feels natural and "right," it's easy to lose track of time and let your mind drift. You're there in body – legs pumping, eyes on the trail ahead – but your mind is free to roam. I really don't recall a half-mile of my walk. To me, nature is a *feeling*, not an environment. It's a feeling you cannot search for, as it mingles with other thoughts. But soon, if you allow it to come on its own terms, an unmistakable sense of peace finds you.

Nature slows you down, putting you in its patient cycle. From that slower pace, you can regain both a lucidity of thought and the perspective often crowded out by the superfluous elements in everyday life. Taking a walk in the woods – a long walk – is often the tonic for what ails you. The combination of the rhythmic physical movement and the quiet setting has therapeutic powers – strong ones that can alter a mood or even a pattern of thought. Nature does not shout for your attention, does not force your eye. She is subtle in letting your thoughts flow free – perhaps even helping to work out a problem in your subconscious.

On this particular winter's day, I had no great problem to solve, but still wished to stay in the woods. The cave at Tantiuesques made me think of Rock House Reservation, where a huge overhang of rock served as shelter for Native Americans. It was just one town north, in West Brookfield, so I drove in that direction and found my way to Route 9.

I was struck by how pleasant a road Route 9 is as it passed through the **Brookfields**, with their lovely town greens, the Benjamin Franklin milestones, and handsome old homes. Was this the same Route 9 that is so hideous to the east in Framingham and Natick? Where consumer madness – fast food, fast oil change, and slow shopping – brings traffic to a crawl? It was, and yet, somehow, it wasn't. Route 9 spans the entire state from Boston to Pittsfield, yet the stretch in the Brookfield area is relatively unknown and unspoiled. Here, you can poke along by choice rather than necessity. With Route 2 bordering the region to the north and the Massachusetts Turnpike to the south, few people have reason to get off the highways.

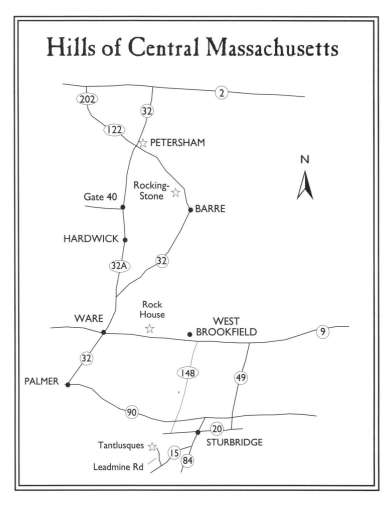

Hills of Central Massachusetts

The **Rock House Reservation** is situated on the north side of Route 9, not far from the intersection with Route 32. On this visit, there seemed to be a couple more inches of snow than down at Tantiusques. I was glad I brought snowshoes. My rule of thumb for snowshoes is that they help when the snow is over eight inches. Under that amount, they seem to require more energy than they save. Snowshoes really come in handy when the ground is covered with a couple of feet of new, powdery snow. Then they allow you to get into bogs, swamps and thick woods you would never explore in other seasons.

The snowshoes made the short walk to the Rock House an easy one. I rested under this unusual stone overhang, thinking of the Native Americans who sat in the same spot so many years ago...

I pictured Indians clothed in animal skins and gathered around a small fire, discussing the forthcoming hunting expedition. While they talked, one of the Indians used a deer antler to chip away at a piece of quartz, the flakes flying off until a perfectly formed arrow head was fashioned. The others looked into the orange flames, each voicing an opinion about the best approach, and the roles they must play to ensure success. Snow was falling, but the rock house kept them dry.

I, too, was dry. Before long, I set out on one of the trails that follows along the side of a small pond. Taking a page from my boyhood, I pretended to be an Indian, walking silently with all senses alert. In the snow I could make out the tracks of deer, a fox, and even a porcupine. How different my pleasurable walk was from the Indian's excursions, which were a matter of survival. And yet I suspect that the hunt itself was an exciting challenge, bringing the possibility of either great satisfaction or deep disappointment. It is said that the Indians had no word for "work," since they considered hunting, growing crops and making tools all part of living, part of the natural cycle in the Great Creator's world.

The trail took me on a ridge above the pond, where there was a little cabin. (I later learned that this would soon house natural history exhibits.) I continued past an unusual glacial boulder resting on a hill, and into woods of oak, maple, pine and hemlock. I walked until my legs ached, then turned back for the car. The "fever" had lifted, and I was ready once more for the cabin.

Winter has its charms in these hills, but with the summer and fall seasons come the country fairs. **Hardwick's** is one of the best. Tents, stalls and old-fashioned games take over the town green, giving you the sense of New England as it was 40 or 50 years ago. I took my kids one year. They loved petting the cows, sheep and pigs, taking the horse and wagon ride, and seeing the little parade. It was a chance to see and feel something on a small scale, something far different than their suburban world.

After the fair I took them to see the **Rockingstone**, actually two massive boulders perched in a seemingly precarious position upon a rock ledge. Despite appearances, the boulders are firmly in place. In fact, they've probably been that way for over 12,000 years, when the retreating glacial sheet deposited them in that exact spot. A face is carved on one of the boulders. This could be as ancient as the cavemen or as recent as a few months ago; the locals I asked about it didn't seem to know.

Rockingstone

The day at the fair was so enjoyable that I came back alone the following day to hike the **Quabbin**. Many people who visit Quabbin Reservoir do so at the **Windsor Dam**, by the visitors' center. Indeed, the views here are spectacular. But this 18-mile-long man-made body of water encompasses 118 miles of shoreline, most of which is open for exploration. One of my favorite access points is Gate 40, where a two-mile walk will bring you past the southern end of Potttapaug Pond (which is connected to the Quabbin), and into the abandoned town green of **Old Dana**. This was one of the towns forced to evacuate when the powers of Boston claimed that a reservoir in the Swift River Valley was more important than the hundreds of homes in Dana, Prescott, Enfield, and Greenwich. These were the towns that were flooded. All that remains of them are old roads and stone walls leading into the dark blue waters of the Quabbin, or some forgotten cellar holes or granite hitching posts hidden in the surrounding forests.

I can't really explain why I'm partial to this spot. Maybe I think that if I visit the Dana green often enough, I'll hear the voices of farmers and mill workers who knew this land when it was cleared for pasture – long before the forest came back to these hills. I've come here on spring evenings and wandered around the triangular green, inspecting old cellar holes and standing inside a hollow tree that reminds me of a boyhood story. There is something enchanting, mysterious, and yet sad about this place that can't be put into words.

On my last visit, I thought I felt the spirits. And maybe I did, because when I returned home from the Quabbin, there was a package waiting for me. Inside was an envelope; I opened this first. It was from a high school friend I had not seen in 10 years. The note said something like, "Thought you might like to read this to your kids; I know how much you love the place." I opened the second package to find a book about the Quabbin, titled *Letting Swift River Go*. The story is that of a woman who recalls a girlhood living happily in the Swift River Valley, and what happened when she and her entire town were forced to leave so the valley could be flooded. How strange that someone I had not heard from in years would send me this particular book on the very day I was at the Quabbin, thinking of the past.

Outside the boundaries of the watershed's forest are other reminders of days gone by. These take the form of moss-covered foundations resting hard by tiny streams and rivers. Mills – long since abandoned with the advent of electricity – were built on just about every moving body of water in this state. The best surviving mills are those made from stone and heavy timber; the stone was often quarried from the very site the mill was to occupy. These buildings were built for functionalism, with Spartan interiors and windows that admitted light but were positioned away from the moving water (which could generate a cold wind). A fireplace or stove was usually placed in the miller's office rather than in the mill room, because of the threat of fire from airborne flour dust.

There is evidence of a mill in a small stream along Route 32A right near Gate 40. There are also signs of abandoned farms – such as the stone walls, so snugly made, that criss-cross the forest. Some of the walls slope down the hillside near the reservoir and disappear into the blue waters of the Quabbin. Though the early settlers certainly didn't build these walls for aesthetic purposes, they are among the finest features of the New England landscape. This is especially true in the fall, when their grey color is a perfect complement to the bare countryside. The settler's stone walls were built from rocks kicked up by the plow; these were convenient materials for both borders and animal pens. To get an idea of just how much of Massachusetts used to be farmland, take a walk in the woods during late autumn after all the leaves have fallen. You will be amazed at the number of stone walls, some of them in mature forests that appear to have been there forever. But the walls tell us otherwise: at the time of their erection, most of this land was agricultural fields and meadows. As settlers migrated to the mid-west in search of better, boulder-free soil, the fields simply reverted to forest.

Today, stone wall construction has become an art. Professional landscapers often charge a handsome price to erect a well-built wall. Contractors often use heavy machinery to excavate a trench and fill it with gravel before actually constructing the wall. This helps prevent the problems caused by frost. The most sought-after rocks for the wall itself are the gray lichen-covered boulders that have weathered for decades. It's rather ironic that many suburban-ites are spending big bucks to have the same rocks that the settlers toiled to remove from their fields trucked to their own land.

The farming that took place in this bony soil is similar to the organic farming that is now making a comeback. Instead of using the pesticides and synthetic fertilizers so common on the post-World War II agribusiness farms, the farms of old New England practiced a natural approach. Weeds were controlled by human labor, a diversity of crops were grown (which meant a diversity of insects), and fields were enriched by manure and ground minerals. There was also a connection with the community, since people knew where their produce was coming from and who grew it. How different from today, when fruits and vegetables come from far-away places such as California or Argentina, rather than from New England.

Now that most of the farmland in central Massachusetts has reverted to woods, you're more likely to see a coyote than a cow. Porcupine are numerous, feeding on the hemlocks. Fishers (a variety of marten) are also present, feeding on the porcupine. Even moose – which just 20 years ago were found only in northern Maine – have pushed westward and southward. Now they inhabit the deep woods around the Quabbin. This last wild area east of the Connecticut River is one we should enjoy, but also protect.

If You Go:

Hardwick Town Hall   (413) 477-6197
    (information on the Hardwick Fair)

Along the Northern Border

Ashby, Ashburnham, Winchendon & Royalston

In north-central Massachusetts – specifically the area between Route 2 and the New Hampshire border – there is not a single tourist destination. It was for this very reason that I took a leisurely weekend drive on the country roads in this often-bypassed area.

Heading northwest on Route 119, I spied the round tops of the two belfries in Ashby and knew that this was a place worth visiting. **Ashby** turned out to be one of those sleepy little towns where bands still play in the gazebo on the village green, and folks stop by just to say hello. While trying to capture the town's beauty on film, I struck up a conversation with a young man who had lived in Ashby all his life. I was surprised to learn that many of the people who lived here had jobs in the high-tech industry, commuting all the way to Route 495. Seems a town that maintains its character and charm can make the long daily drive worth the effort.

I continued my journey through **Ashburnham**, where an old statue caught my attention. Unlike most small-town statues depicting a soldier in arms, this one portrayed a barefoot schoolboy with a book under one arm and a lunch pail in the other. The inscription beneath the statue was perfect. It read: "To a generation of New England boys whose valor in war was equaled only by their achievement in peace."

Ashby

Still stranger structures lay ahead – namely, a huge rocking horse at a fork in the road in downtown **Winchendon**. A sign read: "The Toy Town horse is home again. This is a reproduction of the original Toy Town horse that stood so long in Winchendon and helped identify Winchendon as Toy Town." At the turn of the century, Winchendon was home to the country's largest toy manufacturer, the Morton E. Converse Company. Thus, its nickname.

There was another sign near the horse that was intended to be serious but gave me quite a chuckle. It said that anyone caught climbing the horse was subject to arrest. I laughed, thinking that if I had brought my young children, they would probably have tried to break the law. Only the horse's massive size (it's 20 feet tall) would have prevented them from becoming hardened criminals.

Though the grey horse seemed an odd symbol, I was glad the town remembered its heritage. The fact that one town has a school boy monument, and the next a toy horse, is what makes New England country towns so different in character from those in more developed areas.

Rambling southward a few miles, I came to old **Winchendon Center**. I had been told there was a lovely common here. Indeed, the long triangular green lived up to its billing, having escaped the encroachment of so-called town improvements because of its somewhat remote location. This hilltop village has no general store, no post office, and no gas station. Only an old church and a handful of fine homes – almost every one painted white – encircle the green.

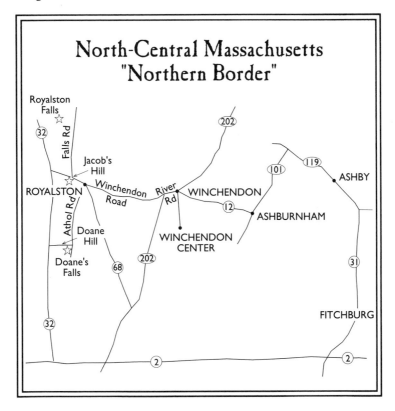

While I walked along the adjacent roads, not a single car passed by, and only a breeze in the trees broke the silence. In front of one house, five large, comfortable-looking wooden chairs faced the green. Did folks here spend the evening hours keeping an eye on their town?

A few minutes later, an elderly man came out of one of the nearby homes and eyeballed me as I was taking notes and shooting pictures. I told him I loved hidden spots, and asked him a couple of questions. He answered in a monotone "yes" or "no," giving me the evil eye all the while. Then he abruptly turned and went back inside.

My guess was that he probably did not appreciate the first "tourist" to inspect the green. I couldn't really blame him; good thing I didn't tell him I was a writer.

I pushed westward into the hills of **Royalston**, where three spectacular waterfalls (and one very interesting outdoorsman/photographer) make this one of my favorite towns.

First, the waterfalls. **Doanes Falls** is at the southern end of town, near the Tully Lake Recreation Area. In the springtime, the water surges through a small granite gorge. Pounding down, it becomes white with foam. Even in summer, when the volume of water decreases, the current is still treacherous and more than one drowning has occurred here. Swimming is not allowed, but hiking along the edge of the falls and Lawrence Brook is a wonderful and safe way to enjoy the area.

Not surprisingly, a mill was situated here as early as 1753. Indeed, its foundation and an old millstone are still visible. Below the falls, the stream's current slows before spilling into 200-acre **Tully Lake**. This is a great spot for boaters, canoeists and campers because of its undeveloped shoreline and many islands. There are only 21 campsites here, so an overnight stop in the 1,000-acre forest at Tully Lake Recreation Area can really give you a feeling of solitude. The dam at the southwestern end of the lake is just one of several in the region constructed to control flooding in the Connecticut River Basin. (Some folks in the region still remember the flood of 1936, and a hurricane that followed two years later, also causing serious flooding.)

Tully Lake adjoins Long Pond, which is really an impoundment on the Tully River. Being a certified "map nut," I have a topographical map of Royalston. I love poring over it, looking for hidden trout streams and old logging roads. One outing I've been meaning to take as a result of this study is a walk from the mouth of Lawrence Brook northward along Tully Lake and Long Pond to Spirit Falls. This map shows a trail that appears to be sandwiched between the water and the shadow of Jacobs Hill.

One of the wonderful things about topographical maps is their ability to trigger daydreams. The terrain often looks so much more interesting on these maps than it is in person. Staring at the brown contour lines of ridges, the green swamps, and the blue waters of backwoods ponds is better than seeing a photograph. For a moment, I feel as though I'm an early explorer, studying a map hand-drawn by Indians. This is especially true with the Royalston Quadrangle, where there are virtually no grey and pink colors denoting developed areas.

From Doanes Falls, I headed north through **Royalston Center,** which I love because of its austere simplicity. The green is not laid out in the traditional manner; it even appeared that Route 68 may have cut through its center. Long sections of grass with old maples line either side of the road, and a lone church with an incredibly high steeple dominates this hilltop village.

The forest comes right to the edge of town, where **Jacobs Hill** provided me with one of the best hikes and views I've had in some time. A 15-minute trek brings you to the edge of a ridge. Here the westward view is one of sky, mountains, and the shimmering waters of Long Pond. Through my binoculars I spied a canoe on the pond below. As I watched the paddlers progress, I wondered if they felt the same exhileration I did in this special place. Sprawled out in the sun, I skimmed a book of nature writing that had been sitting unopened in my pack for more than two years. One passage by Willa Cather seemed to describe the very feeling I had experienced moments earlier when I emerged from the shadow of hemlock woods to this open ridge. "The light air about me told me that the world ended here," she wrote. "Only the ground and sun and sky were left, and if one went a little farther there would be only sun and sky, and one would float off into them, like the tawny hawks which sailed over our heads, making slow shadows on the grass."

Following a trail that extends south along the ridge, I was able to keep the woods to my left and the open air to my right. I recalled an earlier walk on this ridge, when I came upon the tracks of a bobcat. This animal is a solitary meat eater, active mostly at night. His keen hearing and eyesight allow him to lie quietly until his prey happens along. Cottontail and snowshoe rabbits are the bobcat's chief source of food, although he will occasionally eat mice, squirrels, grouse, muskrat and birds. Once in awhile a bobcat will take a young deer – either by stalking, lying in ambush or even positioning himself in a tree above a deer run.

Bobcats den in rock crevices, hollow trees, or under fallen logs, usually mating in February. During this time they make an eerie yowling sound. Their young are born in the early spring and are weaned at two months, remaining with their mother through the summer before going off on their own. If you ever see one, consider it a special wildlife encounter. I'm still waiting for my first glimpse.

Spirit Falls is only a 15-minute walk along this ridge-top trail. Unlike Doanes Falls, this cascading stream splashes rather than roars. Your eye picks up on subtleties such as the dappled light shining on the wet moss. There is no formal trail going down along the falls. If you have the eye of an artist and a penchant for rugged beauty, follow the falls and watch how the water pours off one rock and slides off another, changing from white to grey to green all the while.

Evening wasn't far off when I left Jacobs Hill. I should have headed home, but I couldn't resist driving the three or four miles to Falls Road, where I parked the Subaru and proceeded down the dirt road on foot. A friend had told me Royalston Falls was worth the walk. Since I wasn't sure how long the trek would take, I wondered if I'd be hoofing it out of the woods in the dark. But waterfalls are one of nature's most precious gifts, and I was simply too close not say "Hello."

I almost missed the small sign for the reservation's footpath, but made the turn into the forest nonetheless. Within minutes, I heard rushing water up ahead. The falls themselves were spectacular, plunging about 70 feet in a straight drop to a mist-shrouded pool below. The long day of exploring was taking its toll; I drank mightily from my water jug, then followed a faint trail below the falls, where I dipped my head into the cool water. Mosquitoes harassed me, reminding me that it was late. The light failing, I started back. Something large crossed the path far ahead of me. It was probably a deer, but my imagination suggested mountain lion.

Whatever it was, I thought of calling Paul Rezendes when I got home for the latest report on Royalston wildlife. Rezendes lives in Royalston and is the author of *Tracking & The Art of Seeing.* This fascinating book features superb wildlife photography, interesting anecdotes, tracking instructions, and all the information a person needs to better understand the wild creatures that live around us but often go unseen.

I recall the winter's day on which I first met Rezendes. I was interviewing him when a woman called and asked him to check out some large tracks she had seen in her back yard. We drove to her office to get exact directions. While there, a man who had overheard us talking remarked, "You should check out the bull moose rub I found the other day."

First we drove to the woman's house. It took Rezendes just seconds to realize her error. Smiling through his beard, he pointed to the tracks and said, "She mistook the hopping tracks of a squirrel – where all of its feet land near one another – for the single paw print of a large animal. Happens all the time."

Next we drove to the secluded field where the man said he had seen signs of a moose rub. As we bounced along the country lanes, I asked Rezendes if there really were any moose in the north-central part of our state. "Yes, my wife just saw a big bull the other day," he said. "It seems a few more enter the state from the north each year."

We parked at the edge of the field and started our search. I had forgotten how central Massachusetts often has snow when greater Boston has none, and my sneakers offered little protection from the cold. But as we walked – Rezendes pointing out tracks of a coyote here and a large deer there – I forgot about cold feet and got caught up in the search.

We separated to scan the edge of the field for the tree that bore the markings. "Paul," I shouted, "I found the tree!" It was a small hemlock with a few of its upper branches missing. The top part of its trunk had been stripped of bark.

"Porcupine," said Rezendes. "Let's follow the tracks. These hemlock trees tell quite a story; look at how that one over there is just about dead from years of porcupine feeding. There must be a major denning site nearby." As we followed the pigeon-toed porcupine's trail through the forest, Rezendes identified ruffed grouse tracks. Seconds later, as if on cue, we heard the unmistakable sound of a grouse taking wing.

Rezendes explained that porcupines have a very small range and seldom move out of it. He glanced at my sneakers and noted we could probably find the den within five or 10 minutes. Sure enough, we came upon an area of exposed granite ledges with small caves, nooks and crannies. "This," exclaimed Rezendes with a sweeping gesture, "is a kind of porcupine condominium."

I began to look around more closely and noticed all sorts of signs: droppings, severed hemlock branches, small claw marks on the trunk of a sweet birch, and even a tuft of porcupine fur stuck to a tree. Rezendes stuck his head inside one of the crevices – something I wouldn't have done for a million dollars – and said that had we brought a flashlight, we would probably be able to see the porcupine.

I was kind of glad we had no light.

Leaving the denning area, Rezendes stopped suddenly and exclaimed, "Wait, what do we have here?" Crouching down in the snow for a closer look, he whispered, "The predator has come for the prey." The tracks were those of a fisher cat, the only animal in Massachusetts that actively preys on porcupines. I later learned from Rezendes' book that the fisher kills the porcupine by "continuously circling the animal and lashing out at its head until the porcupine slows down or passes out from loss of blood."

Now, as I walked back to the car in the fading summer light, I reflected on the fact that unplanned events are often the best. If Rezendes and I had stuck to our original plans, we would have missed our search for the bull moose rub, which led to the porcupine hunt. And today, if I had headed straight home from Jacobs Hill, I would have missed the Royalston Falls, the feel of the cold water on my skin, and the glimpse of that mysterious animal that crossed my path.

If You Go:

Tully Lake Campground	(978) 939-8962
Tully Lake Information	(978) 249-9150

The Blackstone River
Valley & Purgatory
Chasm

Sutton, Uxbridge & Northbridge

While Sturbridge Village seems to get all the press (and most of the tourists), the rest of south-central Massachusetts is largely over-looked. Occasionally, I'll come across a passing reference to the town of Webster's linguistic oddity – Lake Chargog-gagoggmanchauggagoggchaubu-nagangamaugg – but the rest of the region hardly gets any mention. Purgatory Chasm (called "New England's Grand Canyon"), Waters Farm, the Blackstone River and Canal Heritage State Park are gems.

Purgatory Chasm State Reservation is off Route 146 in Sutton, Massachusetts. It's only a 40-minute drive from my home in Frank-lin but, like most of us, I rarely see the sights in my own back yard. However, once I did a little research on this geological wonder, I couldn't wait to get there. So I set out early one morning with the intent to explore the canyon.

Arriving at the chasm, I was glad to see only four other cars in the large parking lot. Within five minutes, I was deep inside this great fissure, surrounded by sheer rock walls rising 70 feet above me. It certainly didn't look like the gentle woodlands of central Massachusetts. Since it had a kind of "other-worldly" feel to it, I thought "purgatory" was a good label.

In some respects it reminded me of a gorge without a river in it. The chasm is dry on the bottom and has odd rock formations along its length. It is believed to have been formed when a giant glacial lake released its water and chunks of ice, which tore through this spot. Later, freezing and thawing made the sides split, and rocks tumbled to the bottom of the fissure.

On the floor of the chasm were little caves, great boulders, and jagged outcrops. The hiking was strenuous, and I took my time. I found myself looking upward every few seconds – not so much to see the cliffs above, but to admire some of the largest hemlock trees I've ever seen. (I later learned that a couple of the trees were estimated to be over 300 years old.) I marveled at how these hemlocks grew from the floor of the ravine. How did they find enough soil to sustain themselves? And how did they get enough sunlight when they were smaller?

There were a bunch of young boys having a wonderful time exploring the chasm's many nooks and crannies. In their exuberance, they were making quite a racket. But their voices were contained by the rock walls and as I exited the back end of the chasm, silence filled the woods. Kids are great, but at that moment I preferred the company of two nuthatches that were picking over a hemlock cone.

Having found a sunny spot that offered some warmth on a chilly morning, I sat down to enjoy the solitude. I wondered what the native Indians must have thought about this strange place – was it sacred to them? What legends did they have to explain its origin?

I headed back to my car by walking along the southeastern rim of the ravine. From this vantage point I could see the tops of those massive hemlocks. Strangely, their majesty wasn't quite as awesome now. Maybe a bird's-eye view is not always better.

Back in the parking lot, I met David Podles, Forest and Park Supervisor of Purgatory Chasm. I told him how much I'd enjoyed my visit and that I had never seen anything quite like this place before. That's when he called it the "Grand Canyon of New England." And that's not a bad description. Here in New England, everything seems to be on a much smaller, more intimate

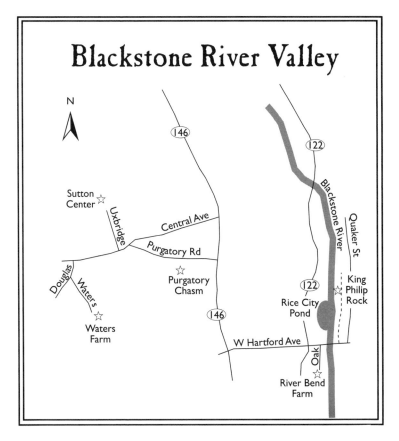

Blackstone River Valley

N

146

122

Sutton
Center

Uxbridge

Central Ave

Purgatory Rd

Douglas

Waters

Purgatory
Chasm

Waters
Farm

146

Blackstone River

Quaker St

122

Rice City
Pond

King
Philip
Rock

W Hartford Ave

Oak

River Bend
Farm

scalethan out West. Maybe a Westernerwould find our geography unimpressive. But for this Yankee, small is beautiful.

From the chasm, I drove a short ways to Uxbridge for a visit to the **Blackstone River and Canal Heritage State Park**. The river was named for William Blaxton, the first European resident of Boston. Blaxton lived alone on the peninsula now known as Boston. That is, until the Puritans infringed on his space. Feeling crowded, Blaxton headed west, away from white men. He ended up settling in this area near the river. It wasn't long before others followed him again and the river was soon the site of many mills, earning it the reputation as "America's hardest working river."

The river begins in the vicinity of Worcester and winds its way southward to Rhode Island's Narragansett Bay. Because it connected Worcester and Providence, the idea for an adjacent canal made perfect sense at the time. Built in 1828, the canal allowed boats to travel the 45 miles between the two cities. (It's incredible to think that the waterway was built with shovels, wheelbarrows, horse and oxen.) Tolls were a penny per mile, per ton of cargo. Canal owners took a long-term view of the project and installed expensive ($4,000 at the time) granite locks rather than the more economical wooden locks. A total of 49 locks were installed, allowing the canal boats to make the series of ascents and descents on their routes. But traffic on the waterway didn't last long. The opening of the Providence and Worcester Railroad in 1848 marked the beginning of the end for the canal, but the mills along the river continued to flourish.

Use of the river had its price. The Blackstone was once one of the most polluted rivers in the country. Not too long ago, the tint of the water indicated the color of the dyes being used in the mills. Yellows, greens, and streaks of red would flow downstream. Today, most of the mills are gone, and local citizens have joined forces with public agencies to restore the river's natural cleanliness. Earnest efforts began with the passage of the Clean Water Act in the 1970s. At that time, the Blackstone River Watershed Association was also formed. Their motto: "We're crazy enough to think the Blackstone River is worth saving!"

Thank God they tried, because today the river has come a long way, and the region seems to have found a new sense of pride. It's heartening to see that, with environmental controls in place, the remaining mills are no longer considered the enemy. And some abandoned mills are being put to good use. Case in point: the old Crown and Eagle Mill on Hartford Street in Uxbridge. After being gutted by fire, the mill was rebuilt as residential housing. Luckily, the building's character was retained and the Blackstone Canal still flows beneath this beautiful and impressive structure.

I parked at a lot off Oak Street in Uxbridge and then took a long walk on the old tow-path that separates the river from the canal. This leads north to the falls at handsome **Stone Arched Bridges**. The newly formed Blackstone River Valley National Heritage Corridor is preserving these scenic spots for all to enjoy. The corridor consists of 20 towns in both Massachusetts and Rhode Island that have historical significance as part of the country's early mill villages. There are plans to build a visitors' center in a 19th-century barn at **Riverbend Farm** (near the parking lot on Oak Street).

Stone Arch Bridge

Each year, more and more visitors are finding their way to this quiet section of the state. Some come for the hiking trails, some for the canoeing, and others for historic sites such as the tremendously scenic **Waters Farm** in nearby West Sutton. Autumn is a particularly popular time; the **Heritage Homecoming** weekend of events is held each October in the corridor's 11 Massachusetts towns.

After exploring the canal, I drove northward to Quaker Street in Northbridge, parking at a small turnoff where a trail leads up to **King Philip Rock**. (You can also reach King Philip Rock via a one-and-a-half-mile trail that begins behind the small office of the Department of Environmental Management on East Hartford Avenue.) From atop the rock, I had a commanding view of both the Blackstone Valley and **Rice City Pond**, which is known for good birding. A friend once told me that he somehow felt energized on overlooks or mountaintops. Resting here, I, too, felt the energy of this quiet place.

Although the rock ledge is named after the Wampanoag Indian leader Metacom (whose English given name was Philip), I wonder if he ever really set foot here. Philip led a war against the settlers beginning in 1675. So many hilltops are named after "King" Philip that I think perhaps the settlers named any Indian gathering spot after him.

While we may never know the truth about Philip's whereabouts, we do know that the white man dug the canal and nature formed the chasm. Both are impressive. Drive out and take a look for yourself.

If You Go:

Blackstone River &
  Canal Heritage State Park   (508) 278-6486
Purgatory Chasm State Park   (508) 234-3733
The chasm is closed whenever snow and ice make it dangerous for walking – usually December through March. The rest of the park is open year-round.

Searching For The Perfect Village Green

Central Massachusetts

What is it about village greens or commons that makes them so appealing? It might be that they recall a simpler time, when neighbor knew neighbor and each town was self-sufficient. Others love them simply for their beauty; each one is an oasis of green at the heart of the town.

Whatever the reason, people who love greens would be lucky indeed to reside in the Bay State – we have more of them than any other state in New England.

Originally, this "common land" was set aside simply because many rural villages in England were configured this way. Here in the New World, they served practical purposes as well. Greens were used as night pasture; settlers kept their sheep and cattle there for protection against wolves.

The cluster of homes around the green also offered a measure of protection from hostile Indians. Later, they were used for militia drills. In the case of Lexington, blood was spilled here, marking the beginning of the Revolutionary War.

In a region of fiercely independent souls, the common ownership of the village green helped hold the towns together. Laws were passed governing their use. Citizens could graze cattle there, but could not cut and sell the grass. Fallen tree limbs could be scavenged for firewood, although the trees themselves could not be touched. In short, the green became the heart of the community, both literally and figuratively.

Time and "progress" have taken their toll on many of our greens. Some now have roads criss-crossing them, while others have been slowly consumed by blacktop to the point where they are little more than traffic islands. But a few towns have preserved their greens, thereby maintaining the dignity and heritage of the town itself.

My favorite greens all convey a sense of peace and tranquility. And the structures that surround them are important, too. A white church, town hall, library, post office, and general store all rank high in my book, especially if the buildings predate this century. Signs of the past (such as a stone wall, hitching post, pump or horse trough) can only help. Signs of the present (such as a convenience store or gas station) can only hurt.

If there is a neon sign, I don't even stop the car.

Trees also play a critical role. Too few, and the common looks forlorn and barren. Too many, and it resembles a park. The size of the trees makes a difference, as well. One towering sugar maple with a spreading canopy of leaves can really win me over. I feel the same about bandstands or gazebos, especially if made completely from wood and painted white with a uniquely shaped weather vane on top.

A good green makes me want to stop and wander around, looking for historical markers or reading inscriptions on monuments. If it's a nice warm day, perhaps I'll munch on an apple, lay out in the grass, and chat with the first person that happens by.

The most beautiful of all village greens are located in central Massachusetts. Many are just a few minutes' drive from Worcester.

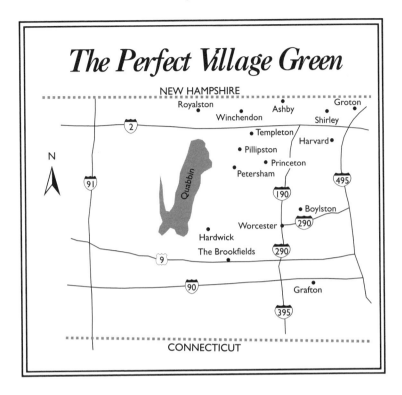

The Perfect Village Green

NEW HAMPSHIRE

Royalston
Ashby
Groton
Winchendon
Shirley

2

Templeton
Harvard
Pillipston
Princeton
Petersham

N

91

Quabbin

190

495

Boylston
Worcester
290

Hardwick
The Brookfields
290

9

90

Grafton

395

CONNECTICUT

North Of Route 2

There are a number of fine greens in the towns north of Route 2. One winter, I visited **Old Shirley Center** (north of the "downtown" Shirley) at twilight. Enjoying the peace and quiet, I also admired a spectacular pink-streaked horizon to the west. Old homes from the Federal period gave the place a solid look, as did the monument dedicated to the men that "hazarded their lives to suppress the Great Rebellion." On one side of the green is the First Parish Meeting House (1773). An adjacent town "pound" boasts five-foot stone walls and an ancient entry gate, complete with rusted lock. (This is where stray cattle were kept until their owners came to retrieve them.) Nearby is the town hall with its massive white columns. Originally constructed in 1848, it was rebuilt in 1950 after being struck by lightning.

Groton has a small green in front of the beautiful First Parish Church (1755). This is surrounded by a fence constructed of granite posts with wooden rails. The historic Inn at Groton is situated next to the green. Here, an ancient stone marker points east, with the inscription "To Boston 35."

The little town of **Ashby** – set along the New Hampshire border – has a fine green surrounded by two churches, a burial ground, and a weathered old grange hall. On the green itself is a gazebo, an old hand pump, a monument to the early settlers, and a couple of ancient gnarled maples.

Just to the west of Ashby is **Old Winchendon Center**. Situated south of the main part of town, this features a long triangular green spread between quiet backroads. Almost all the old homes surrounding the green are painted white, adding to its simple beauty.

Still further north (and west of Route 2) is **Royalston**. Though off the beaten path, this town's impressive hilltop green is worth a visit. Located in front of both the old town hall and a church with an extremely tall steeple, it has an austere look to it. The land surrounding the green is so wild-looking that it's easy to imagine a time when the town was still vulnerable to Indian attacks.

South Of Route 2

The area south of Route 2 – in the central part of the state – has a wide variety of preserved town greens. Not far from Route 495 is the town of **Harvard**, which has somehow managed to keep development at bay. Indeed, its sloping green is picture-perfect. The Unitarian Church sits at one end, while at the other are a general store, library and another church. One of this green's best features is an old millstone with an inscription explaining when the town was established.

Princeton has a charming hilltop green, reminiscent of some of those in Vermont and New Hampshire. Two stone buildings at the high end of the green give it a feeling of permanence and grace. **Boylston** also has two handsome stone structures; the Sawyer Library looks like it was made from different kinds of rock, while the town hall is made from huge blocks of Boylston granite.

Grafton's common has such a typical New England feel that the site was used in the motion picture version of Eugene O'Neill's *Ah, Wilderness!* It features no fewer than three churches, as well as a host of buildings dating back to the 1800s. One of these is an awesome, well-maintained Victorian structure. Surrounding the common is a fence of wooden railings supported by granite posts and a number of large shade trees. Historic signs abound. One at the Country Store reads, "John Eliot established here in 1651 a village of Christian Indians called Hassanameset –'at the place of small stones.' It was home to James the Printer, who helped Eliot print the Indian bible."

On one of my visits to Grafton, I met Carolyn Pfau, who has lived here since 1917. She told me some of the history of the green, noting that in the 1800s, all the trees here had been cut down for firewood or to make room for pastures. She declared, "The green is always threatened by development, but I'm here to protect it!" Amen.

Grafton

West Brookfield has a very large green – so large, in fact, that one portion of it houses a baseball diamond. This 3½-acre common also contains a large bandstand, in which free concerts are held during the summer. At one end of the green is a milestone laid by Benjamin Franklin. (He set them along the Old Post Road in the days when postage was paid by the mile.) Just down the road, Brookfield's smaller common is quieter, because it sits back off Route 9.

The region east of Quabbin Reservoir is replete with wonderful villages apparently frozen in time. Both **Petersham** and **Hardwick** have classic village greens. Hardwick's is encircled by an old-fashioned general store, a post office, two churches, and a town hall that resembles a church. And this is a working green. Every August, livestock invades the open space for the **Hardwick Fair** – a wonderful event, especially for children. Petersham's green has a number of stately buildings with white columns in the Greek Revival style. This gives the center something of a regal, 18th-century look. Benches and a gazebo invite you to stop and rest a spell. If you happen to be in the area on a Sunday, stay for the evening concert on the green.

Just north of Petersham are two more interesting greens. The center of **Phillipston** is a tiny place, dominated by the 1785 Congregational Church with its ancient wooden clock. Nearby **Templeton** has a larger town center, complete with an "Ice Cream Barn and Antique Store" in an old white building alongside the crossroads.

Every town should be lucky enough to have "common land" at its heart.

Eastern
Massachusetts

The Overlooked Coast

Dartmouth & Westport

It was a warm summer evening, but along the shorefront of Westport and Dartmouth, a weak breeze blew cooling ocean air from Rhode Island Sound. I was exploring **Allen's Pond**, a little-known refuge owned by the Massachusetts Audubon Society. Walking the crescent-shaped beach that separates the ocean from the pond, I lifted my binoculars to scope a large bird winging by.

The pond is a nesting site for one of nature's most beautiful birds, the osprey. These large fish-eating predators are still somewhat uncommon in New England, due to loss of habitat and the effects of DDT on their reproduction. But with the banning of the pesticide and the establishment of sanctuaries like Allen's Pond, the osprey have been making a gradual comeback. They can be identified by the crook in their long wings and the black "wrist" marks. Seeing them hunt is remarkable: first they hover far above their prey, then they plunge feet-first into the water, using their talons to snatch an unsuspecting fish.

I first learned about ospreys at the **Lloyd Center for Environmental Studies** in Dartmouth. Kids will love this place; the main building contains aquariums and exhibits that feature live fish, turtles and snakes. The center is small, but it has a homey feel and the staff is available to answer questions. They will let children look through the birding scope on the top floor, which offers a panoramic view of the Slocums River and the tidal waterways below. Nature trails wind through the center's 55 acres of rich and diverse habitats. These include freshwater wetlands, a salt marsh and an oak-hickory forest.

As I walked the shore at Allen's Pond, I noticed the breeze had died completely. I was ready to take a dip. On a whim, I went straight to **Horseneck Beach**, even though the light was fading. Here the air felt thick and heavy, with dark ominous clouds approaching from the south. But I couldn't resist the ocean. I walked into the surf, swimming beyond the breaking waves to float on my back.

Oh, the joy of being in the water! It was both soothing and energizing at the same time. The salt water seemed to sweep away a few years, and I played in the waves, the roar of the surf around me.

I was the only fool in the ocean. In fact, I could see only two other people on the beach. "Why don't I do this more often?" I wondered. The water felt so good, and the sky was so beautiful: a mix of slate grey clouds billowing to the south, and to the west a bit of pink. Evening or early morning – not the heat of the day – is the perfect time for the shore.

I was in the water so long that the tide came up a bit. When I got out, I couldn't find my pack. Panic shot through me; glasses, wallet, and car keys gone – and I'd barely begun the trip.

Squinting, I combed the beach. Far to my left, a dark object sat on the sand. I sprinted toward it. Relief – the pack was safe. While swimming, the waves had carried me far down the beach.

Water marks extended 20 feet on either side of the pack, indicating spots where the waves had rolled up. Amazingly, the pack itself was dry. I flopped down in the sand and laughed; a good omen for this two-day ramble.

Fifteen minutes later I arrived at **Salt Marsh Farm Bed & Breakfast**. Even in the dim twilight I knew I'd made the right choice. The 1727 farmhouse sits behind a stone wall, with fields all around it. I went to a side door and knocked. Owner Sally Brownell welcomed me in, giving me a quick tour. Wide pine floorboards – a bit uneven – creaked beneath us as we passed through low doorways. The wood on which we were treading was undoubtedly growing before the white man took over these coastal plains. Indeed, the home seemed alive with history.

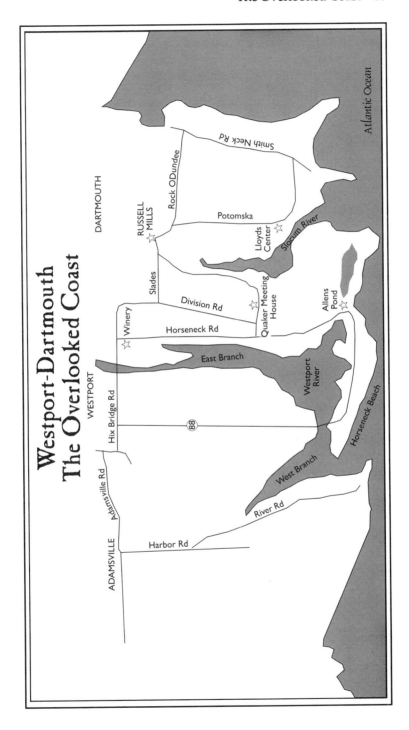

Westport-Dartmouth
The Overlooked Coast

The next morning I lingered in bed, enjoying its comfort. Suddenly, the aroma of perking coffee caught my attention and I headed downstairs. Sally was in the kitchen and she poured me a cup. While she cooked breakfast, I wandered into the living room. This is where I noticed that we owned many of the same books. There was a whole shelf on the history of various towns along Rhode Island Sound and Buzzards Bay. At the end of the row I saw a book that made me smile: *The Diary of King Philip's War* by Colonel Benjamin Church, the colonist's most celebrated and successful Indian fighter. So I wasn't the only one intrigued by this war. I shouted out to Sally that her book collection was top-notch, and that Church's book was one of my favorites.

Over a breakfast of pancakes and bacon, Sally outlined sites I should visit. She marked the spots on my map, after which we carried our coffee outside, wetting our feet on the morning dew. A giant elm tree had survived in her side yard and we sat beneath it, falling into easy conversation. I asked her about the bed and breakfast business, for which she seemed a "natural." Her reply was an enthusiastic one: "Oh, I love meeting all the interesting people, and sharing our love for this region with them." When asked about the drawbacks, she said that the only one is being tied to the house.

I looked around me, the sun climbing over the field and a breeze rustling through the elm above. If you had to be tied somewhere, this was a good place. I thought how rarely I'd had the time to enjoy a morning so fully, and to notice subtle things such as the early sunlight striking a mighty elm.

As we walked through the yard, I commented on the variety of trees. Maples, beech, oak, red cedar and birch were all within sight. Bittersweet climbed the rock wall and high-bush blueberries grew nearby. Sally stopped at a plant with small yellow flowers, breaking off a stem and rubbing it on her arm. "Jewelweed," she said. "If you ever get poison ivy, just rub this on." I made a mental note of what the plant looked like and commented how we probably learned of its medicinal use from the Indians. I wonder how much we have already forgotten from those who knew this land in a way that we never will.

Once the car was packed, I waved goodbye. With rumors of modern-day Wampanoags and the state of Massachusetts becoming partners in a gambling casino in adjacent New Bedford, I wonder if my next visit will find the place changed for the worse.

There are a number of secluded villages in this area. One of my favorites is **Russells Mills Village**, with its 1871 white school-house, doll museum, and waterfall by an old mill site. Small cranberry bogs can be seen on the backroads. These are especially beautiful in the fall, when the crimson berries are harvested. The towns of southeastern Massachusetts, including Cape Cod, produce almost half of the country's cranberry crop.

View from Horseneck Road

I explored the village, then headed south. Surprisingly, dairy farms are still widely scattered throughout the region. At the **Old Quaker Meeting House** on Horseneck Road I watched a farmer trying to herd a cow out of the graveyard. The cow was not cooperating, because the grass in the graveyard was thicker than that in the field. For a moment I thought about going to help. But then I saw the horns on the cow and decided my role was to photograph the proceedings, which had taken on something of a comic air as the cow repeatedly out-maneuvered the farmer. A neighbor finally arrived and together they got the job done, while I took pictures from a safe distance.

The Quakers used their Meeting House for "gatherings of worship without fixed religious rituals." That concept appeals to me, but I would not have wanted to be a Quaker during the 1600s. The Puritan colonists were barbaric in their treatment of those who held differing beliefs. More than one Quaker had his or her tongue pierced by a hot iron spike at the hands of the Puritans.

Southeastern Massachusetts and Rhode Island were a stronghold for Quakers before the settling of Pennsylvania. Roger Williams, the founder of Providence, Rhode Island, believed in religious freedom. As Puritan intolerance intensified, many Quakers fled or were banished from Massachusetts Bay Colony and subsequently settled in Rhode Island. The Quakers originally called themselves Friends. It is reported that the term "Quaker" has its origins in ridicule, being a sarcastic description of the way the Friends were said to tremble with religious feeling at their gatherings.

In many respects, the Quakers were ahead of their time. Both men and women were permitted to speak at meetings, and they believe that God's "inner light" may come to any individual, even non-Christians. Long before Thoreau and Gandhi, the Quakers were practicing their own unique form of civil disobedience by ignoring the Puritan government and following their own faith.

Their austere meeting houses are handsome in their simplicity. But to my eye, the stone walls that invariably surround them are a real source of beauty. The time and effort that went into building these old walls must have been enormous. Considering how much frost can damage them, I'm always amazed to find so many walls still in perfect shape, with level tops. One such wall – just north of here, in Acushnet – is constructed from massive stone blocks that fit together almost perfectly. The few cracks are filled with smaller stones so that no light can filter through. Walls like this one are more than mere property markers or boundaries for livestock; surely these are works of art, built with quiet pride. If a person can love an inanimate thing, then for me, it's a stone wall.

Nearby I spied another well-constructed stone wall, this one used to keep horses corralled. The scene was so striking that I stopped and fished my camera out of my pack. A rolling field of green grass angled down toward the golden salt marsh surrounding an estuary. A black horse galloped over to me and I took picture after picture, the whole time thinking that this was once Indian land. It was not until I put the camera down that I realized the crescent-shaped beach below was Allen's Pond. How did I miss this scene yesterday? Sometimes heaven is right in front of us, while our minds are in the clouds.

And so I followed the stone walls, heading north past corn, dairy cows and fields of tall grass. Much of this coastal land now supports thriving vineyards. At the east branch of the Westport River, I followed the sign for the **Westport Rivers Winery.**

Laid out neatly on a gentle hillside, these vineyards overlooked the river, with row after row of green vines stretching to the west. I immediately hit it off with owners Bob and Carol Russell, who told me that they had purchased the farm 14 years ago. "How did you happen to get into the business?" I asked, thinking of the risks involved in such a venture.

Carol looked at Bob. Smiling, she replied, "It's probably in the blood. Both (sets of) grandparents had wineries, but we knew little about the business. We lived in a nearby suburban area; Bob was working 70 hours a week and traveling. One Christmas I gave him a wine-making kit, and one thing led to another, with Bob first planting vines in the back yard."

Bob warmed to the story, adding, "It was a big decision. We still had a 10-year-old and teenagers when we made the plunge. But it seemed like a good way for the entire family to spend more time together, and I've always had an entrepreneurial spirit."

I shook my head in wonder. So many of us – myself included – don't dare cut the cord from a "safe" life to pursue a dream. People like the Russells fascinate me. Largely self-educated about a new venture, they simply decide the time is right to get out and sail on uncharted waters. I'm fascinated... and a bit envious.

Carol took me through the farmhouse, explaining that she and Bob direct the business aspects of the winery, while sons Bob Jr. and Bill grow the grapes and make the wine. The restored 19th-century Victorian farmhouse reminded me a bit of Salt Marsh Farm, and I told Carol how much I loved it. "A number of architects we interviewed for the restoration process told us it was hopeless and we should tear it down," she said. "But the history is one reason we fell in love with this place."

Tear it down! The thought made me sick. Maybe I was reacting a bit strongly, because my favorite covered bridge – the oldest one in Massachusetts – had recently been torched by some degenerate kids. And a new covered bridge in Foster, Rhode Island, went up in flames the same way. I'm sure when these kids are caught they'll receive a cursory slap on the wrist, and continue on their merry destructive ways. I say bring the public stocks back, erect them on the village green, and keep those arsonists in them until they walk with a permanent hunch. And while I'm venting my rage, I think that their parents should be placed in the stocks next to them. I have kids, too, but I'll take my chances.

Carol never knew the thoughts that raced through my mind as we walked outside and into the vineyards. Here she explained how the ocean is what makes all this possible. It extends the growing season by providing milder temperatures in the winter, while during the summer the coastal breezes keep the grapes dry and free of rot. "I love it here in the winter," she said, making a sweeping gesture with her arm. "The sunlight on the river lights up like diamonds, and the hoar frost give the vines a silvery look with everything in bare-bones simplicity."

I bought a bottle of chardonnay and pushed on, glad for the open spaces the wineries have saved. Besides, it's good to use the products of our own New England soil; so much of what we consume today comes from hundreds of miles away.

Back in the car, I studied my map closely. I wanted to go to a tip of Westport that is cut off by the west branch of the Westport River. I realized that to reach this section of Massachusetts, I had to go into Rhode Island and then veer back to the southeast.

Crossing the state line, I passed two weather-worn buildings, one with a sign reading **Gray's Gristmill**. I decided to turn around, park and walk inside.

A young man came out of the little shop adjacent to the mill. "Would you like to see it?" he asked. I introduced myself and he took me inside. As soon as the door opened and the scent of flour poured over me, I was transported back to my father's bakery in Springfield, Massachusetts. It's amazing what the sense of smell can do; within a split second, I could actually feel my father's presence. I could see him scraping dough out of the mixer, dropping it into the enormous greased tub. I saw my brother and I as small boys, perched atop a skyscraper of flour bags, eating our lunches and watching my father and the others work, joke, and argue with words not heard at home.

The flashback – if that's what you call it – was over in a second. I took a big breath, trying perhaps to keep the flour scent close to my soul. We walked to the back window, where the miller, Tim, pointed to an ancient tractor outside. "That's what powers the mill; the water power just wasn't enough," he said. "But the millstone down below, and this building itself – they're originals. In fact, so is the General Store next door. It was built in 1788. You ought to go see it."

I did. Again, waves of emotion and boyhood memories came flooding over me. The store – which hadn't been modernized much – resembled my grandfather's little grocery store from long ago. Old shelving, wooden floor boards, ancient display cases and faded signs – it was as if I'd walked back in time. I thought back on my grandfather, with his slow ways, his big belly, and his pride in that store. But then the supermarkets came, siphoning off his customers and breaking his spirit in the process. The store closed; within a couple of years, Grandpa had a stroke and was never the same.

A few feet down the road, I was pleasantly surprised to discover the unique-looking village of **Adamsville**. Instead of a town green, there is a baseball diamond in its center; instead of a white steepled church, there is "the tower"; and instead of a Civil War statue, there's a monument to a chicken.

First, the chicken. This may surprise you, but I'm an expert on monuments to chickens. This **monument to the Rhode Island Red** – which commemorates the establishment of that breed here in 1854 – is purported to be the country's only monument to a chicken in the United States. However, I recall seeing something similar on a night of carousing in Gainesville, Georgia. Though I'll admit things were a little blurry, I swear I saw a statue of a chicken atop a tall stone pillar. If you're ever in north Georgia, check it out for yourself.

The Tower at Adamsville is an old water tower that has been converted to a gift shop. (It actually looks like a windmill, without the wheel of blades.) Inside, I chatted with the owner and asked directions to the western tip of Westport.

Following her advice, I turned down a beautiful old lane called Westport Harbor Road. Here I spied egrets, heron and osprey over a marsh. This road turns into River Road, passing back into West-port before ending abruptly at the ocean. I turned left down a dirt road, which also came to an end. Ahead was a huge mound of rock, and I hoofed it to the top. There I sat and watched the sun set over the mouth of the Westport River – all the while thinking of Quakers, tides, and ospreys.

If You Go:

Westport Rivers Winery	(508) 636-3423
Salt Marsh Farm Bed & Breakfast	(508) 992-0980
Lloyd Center for Environmental Studies	(508) 990-0505

Thoreau Country

Concord, Lincoln & Weston

To paraphrase our resident sage, Henry David Thoreau, I have traveled far in Concord. On this outing, we will explore some of the more celebrated sites, as well as a few of the lesser-known byways.

Thoreau enthusiasts come from far and wide to make the pilgrimage to **Walden Pond**. But on a summer's day, it's hardly the quiet place old Henry knew. If you're looking to capture his spirit, your best bet is to take a walk around the pond in the early morning. Or better still, visit Thoreau's grave site at Sleepy Hollow Cemetery on Bedford Street. On a hillside known as **Author's Ridge,** some of the best minds in America were laid to rest. The graves of Alcott, Hawthorne, Thoreau, and Emerson are all situated in this peaceful spot.

On my first visit to the old burial ground, I was expecting a large headstone by Thoreau's grave. Instead, I found a small slab that simply said "Henry." Nearby was a larger headstone listing all the Thoreaus who are laid to rest here. Knowing how much Henry loved his family, I was moved to pay my respects, recalling all the pleasure I've had reading his work over the years. I particularly remembered Henry's special relationship with his older brother John. The two young men were teachers together. They also traveled the countryside together, as chronicled in *A Week On The Concord and Merrimack*. John died just three years after their river journey, and the book was Henry's memorial to his brother.

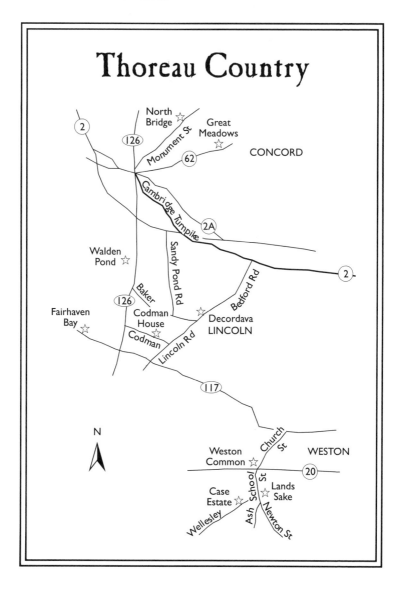

Like most writers, Henry Thoreau experienced problems finding a publisher. After many rejections, he decided to print the book at his own expense. Four years later, with only a couple of hundred books sold, the printer returned the rest to him. That Thoreau found a way to tell this sad story with a bit of humor is one reason I find him so fascinating. In his journal he wrote, "I have now a library of nearly 900 volumes, over 700 of which I wrote myself."

At the **Concord Museum** – and also in the parking area by Walden Pond – are replicas of Thoreau's Walden cabin. This he built himself, enjoying every minute of the process. He wrote, "Shall we forever resign the pleasure of construction to the carpenter?" As Thoreau's cabin only measured 10 by 15 feet, the materials cost him little more than $28. Far from becoming a hermit at Walden, Thoreau often entertained visitors at his cabin or made the short walk into town to dine with his family. (Should you visit Walden Pond, his cabin was located on the north side – on your right, facing the pond from the beach area).

This may sound obsessive, but over the years I've read *Walden* five or six times – never ceasing to be amazed at how Thoreau had pinpointed exactly what ails us. He wrote, "It appears as if men had deliberately chosen the common mode of living because they preferred it to any other. Yet they honestly think there is no choice left. But alert and healthy natures remember that the sun rose clear. It is never too late to give up our prejudices." Later, he commented on those who "give up" today in the hope of accumulating wealth to enjoy later. "No doubt they can ride at last who shall have earned their fare, that is, if they survive so long, but they will probably have lost their elasticity and desire to travel by that time." It's fortunate that Thoreau followed his own advice, because he died in his 40s. He had certainly lived for the day, pursuing his passions and ignoring society's pressure to produce in a more traditional way.

Thoreau's good friend Emerson (who owned the plot of land where Henry built his cabin) also lived in Concord. His primary homes were the Old Manse, by the historic North Bridge, and the Emerson House, on the Cambridge Turnpike. He lived at **Emerson House** from 1835 to his death in 1882, producing some of his finest work there. His personal effects, furniture and book collection are on exhibit at this house, which is open to the public seasonally. Thoreau spent a year living here as well – exchanging his gardening and handyman skills for room and board.

The Old Manse was home not only to Emerson, but to Nathaniel Hawthorne. This writer lived there for a two-year period, beginning on his wedding night in 1842. These were happy times for Hawthorne and his bride Sophia. While he wrote in the upstairs study, she painted in the studio. Later in the day, both walked the grounds or tended the gardens. From their back windows, they looked over the pasture and down to the Concord River. The river drew Hawthorne like a magnet; he spent many early mornings fishing and bringing his catch back for breakfast. It was Thoreau who taught him to row, even selling him a boat. Hawthorne recognized Thoreau's skills as an outdoorsman, writing, "Mr. Thoreau managed the boat so perfectly... that it seemed instinct with his own will, and to require no physical effort."

The Old Manse is situated in an unforgettable setting featuring gardens, large trees and meadows. It's also adjacent to one of the most historic spots in America, the **Old North Bridge**. As every schoolboy knows, this was the site of the first battle of the American Revolution. On the morning of April 19, 1775, roughly 400 "Minutemen" waited here for the British. A brief battle ensued, with the Minutemen routing the Redcoats, who had to run a gauntlet of armed colonials all the way back to Boston. Near the bridge is the grave site of two British soldiers who died there. At the bridge's western end is the famous Minuteman Statue by Daniel Chester French.

Old North Bridge

Be sure to visit the **North Bridge Visitor Center**, part of the Minuteman National Historical Park. Located on the west side of the bridge, the center was built in 1911 as a private home near Punkatasset Hill (the high point where the colonial militia gathered before the battle). It now houses exhibits and activities relevant to the events of April 19, 1775. The center's grounds burst into spectacular color in the spring, with rhododendron, azaleas, mountain laurel, and all sorts of flowering perennials and annuals. To reflect on the power of the place, stroll the grounds at dawn on a spring morning. Another way to experience the Old North Bridge is to rent a canoe at the **South Bridge Boathouse** and paddle to the Old North Bridge.

It takes some imagination to hear "the shot heard round the world," because today the scene is the picture of peace and tranquility. The slow-moving waters of the Concord River pass beneath the wooden bridge, and the only sound is that of bird calls from the woods and meadows. **The Concord River** – immortalized in the writing of Thoreau – starts just a short way upstream from the Old North Bridge, at the juncture of the Assabet and the Sudbury Rivers. Perhaps the best way to see the wildlife that abounds here is to visit **Great Meadows Wildlife Refuge**. A great walk at the refuge is just a couple of miles from the Old North Bridge, off Route 62 on Monson Road. Here you will find both an observation tower and a well-groomed trail that spans a dike between two ponds and follows the river. It's an especially good area for children; the trails are flat, it's almost impossible to get lost, and the chances of seeing birds such as ospreys, great blue herons and wood ducks are excellent. If you're lucky, you might even spot snakes and turtles basking in the sun's warming rays.

The center of Concord is very walkable, with shops, old colonial homes, and a plethora of historic sites such as **Wright Tavern**. The latter was the headquarters of the Minutemen early on April 19th, 1775; later that same day, the British commanders operated from there. Take a stroll down Lexington Road to see more fine structures from the 18th century. On your way, remember that Thoreau considered walking an art. He wrote, "I have met but one or two persons in the course of my life who understood the art of walking, that is, of taking walks – who had a genius, so to speak, for *sauntering*." So take your time, let your curiosity lead you, and learn the art of sauntering.

Just outside the town center – where Lexington Road and the Cambridge Turnpike merge – is the **Concord Museum**. Besides containing many of Thoreau's and Emerson's possessions, it showcases Native American artifacts and relics from the Revolution. You can see one of the lamps hung from the Old North Church and musket flints discarded on that first bloody day of the Revolution.

There are 15 period rooms displaying items from Concord's past, including Emerson's library. Of special interest to me is the Thoreau Gallery Room, which features artifacts from both his sojourn at Walden Pond and his parent's home. Included are his desk, bed, chair, surveying tools and flute.

A bit farther east on Lexington Road are two more interesting sites that are open to the public. Known as the "home of the authors," **The Wayside** housed the Hawthornes, the Lothrops, and Louisa May Alcott, who based her novel *Little Women* on some of her girlhood experiences here. Alcott later lived at the **Orchard House**. This is where she actually wrote the novel, despite suffering from mercury poisoning. (The latter was brought on by medication used to treat the typhoid she had contracted years earlier, while a nurse in Washington.)

There are many more points of interest in Concord, and brochures can be picked up at the Concord Museum. Sometimes the best way to see a town is from a bicycle; on many a Sunday morning I've pedaled the backroads, thankful for the open space around me. But I've also seen the past 25 years' development slowly nibble away at woods and fields where I once stopped to hike. As I cycle through Concord's backroads, I know full well what Thoreau meant when he wrote, "I was born in the most favored spot on earth – and just in the nick of time, too."

Neighboring **Lincoln** and **Weston** are also worthy of exploration. If the idea of a bike ride appeals to you, **Lincoln Guide Service** on Lincoln Road is a good choice for rentals. It's also located near backroads that are great for biking. One of these is Codman Road, which is lined by huge shade trees, fields and stone walls. Stop at the historic **Codman House**, an impressive country estate with a commanding view of the surrounding fields. The house has a multi-layered character reflecting numerous alterations made over the years. It features elements from the Georgian, Federal, Victorian, and Colonial Revival periods. Surrounding the home is an English cottage garden and an Italianate garden with fountains, reflecting pools, terracing, and statues.

Cyclists can make a small loop through this Lincoln section by following Codman Road to its intersection with Route 126, and then proceeding north to **Baker Bridge Road** on the right. This is another country road that's just begging to be explored. About halfway down, you'll notice a unique structure called the **Gropius House**. This was built in 1938 by one Walter Gropius, a leading proponent of modern architecture. Gropius built this home for his family, combining traditional New England architectural elements – such as clapboard and fieldstone – with glass block, chromed banisters, and welded steel. The house's design makes good use of the surrounding landscape, with screened porches and large plate glass windows. Though shaded by overhangs in the summer, these windows admit enough sunlight in the winter to brighten up the interior.

Turn right at the western end of Baker Bridge Road, continuing your loop onto Sandy Pond Road and toward the **Decordova Museum**. This unique museum and 35-acre sculpture park rest high on rolling lawns and woodlands above Sandy Pond, offering a nice combination of art and the outdoors. Continuing eastward on Sandy Pond Road, you'll arrive at the center of **Lincoln**. This is a charming spot to walk about and examine the beauty of some fine old homes. I especially like the Lincoln Public Library, housed in an old brick building with an odd-looking twisted tree out front. Follow Lincoln Road south out of town to complete the loop.

Another interesting town is neighboring **Weston**, which has an expansive bowl-shaped green and acres of open space. This town is home to many of Massachusetts' rich and famous, but visitors can enjoy biking the backroads, viewing the gardens at the Case Estates, or walking the miles of nature trails scattered throughout town.

Because it's only a few miles from Boston, you wouldn't think Weston could be the site of one of my most unusual wildlife encounters, but it is. I was walking beneath some grand old hemlocks one spring afternoon. Up ahead, I could hear crows calling the way the they do when agitated. Sure enough, around a bend, I saw a number of crows. Seconds later, I saw the object of their harassment: a great horned owl. Surprisingly, the owl did not fly off when I appeared. I therefore had the pleasure of observing it closely through binoculars.

When I turned to go, something white directed my eye toward the ground. At the base of a hemlock was a baby owl, about seven inches long and covered in pure white down. Standing on its legs, it twisted its head to watch me as I circled it. An owl that size and color can only be about four weeks old; I assumed it must have fallen out of its nest.

Not wanting the parent to swoop down and strafe me, I kept my distance and watched the baby through my binoculars. Even at this age, its talons were quite large. It clicked its beak a couple of times, probably to let the mother know it felt threatened. I backed away and left the woods.

The next day I returned to find the baby still there but the mother nowhere in sight. This was a disturbing development, because the mother usually continues to feed the baby even if it has fallen from the nest. I maintained my distance, knowing that though the mother may be out of sight, she could swoop down at any minute. Owls can fly silently and surprise unsuspecting prey because their wings are well-padded with soft, velvety feathers. If the fledgling's talons were impressive, I could only imagine what the mother's looked like.

By the third and fourth days, it became clear that the mother was gone. It had rained for two days and the baby looked miserable, barely moving when I approached. Its white down was matted and it didn't even hiss or snap its beak, only watching me through half-open eyes.

I made a few phone calls, and through the Department of Environmental Management found wildlife rehabilitators who agreed to look at the baby. Confirming that the owlet was starving, they took it to their center, where it was raised until old enough to fend for itself.

Trail maps of Weston's conservation land can be purchased at the town hall. These give directions to numerous parcels set aside for walking. The land surrounding Hobbs Brook and Hobbs Pond is especially scenic, as is the forest of cedar and pine encircling the Weston Reservoir. The walk around the reservoir takes about 40 minutes and is a good one for the summer because most of the trail is shaded.

But the real gems of Weston, to my way of thinking, are **Land's Sake** and the **Case Estates**. Managed by the Arnold Arboretum, the Case Estates are a combination of display gardens and woodland trails. These are lined with a wide variety of trees, flowers and shrubs, mixed with plants that have grown naturally. Many of the plantings have special labels, making them a convenient source of ideas for the home gardener.

Spring and early summer are the best months to visit. During this time, you can walk the woodland paths beneath towering pines and observe delicate pink lady's-slippers contrasting with the darker shades of the forest floor. Azaleas, rhododendrons, and blooming dogwoods are particularly vivid in their annual displays of color. Herb gardens, ground covers, and extensive nurseries are laid out beautifully around the old barn and schoolhouse at the front of the property.

One of the estate's most interesting features is a massive stone wall. Ten feet in height, it is said to be New England's longest free-standing dry wall of native stone. Daylilies grow in its shadow, while more tender plants thrive in the protection of its southern base. A path from the gardens winds invitingly past an old gate in the wall and into the dark woods.

Nearby are a series of open fields, one of which is used by Land's Sake. This is a non-profit organization that uses a portion of the land along Newton Street to grow organic fruits and vegetables. Feel free to wander along these paths, observing various gardening practices. If it's been years since you enjoyed the scent of freshly turned earth, come walk these fields in the spring. It's during this season that the natural world seems bursting with energy. Birding and wildlife sightings are also good here; I often spot bluebirds and red-tailed hawks. On my last walk, I noted a problem common to many gardens: groundhogs. No matter how hard you try to rid your land of these pests, groundhogs always seem to have the last laugh.

A meadow near the crop fields contains some truly beautiful trees. There are specimens of mountain ash, weeping willow, golden larches, magnolias, and sugar maples, but my favorites are two spectacular European beeches. The view over the trees from Newton Street is a landscape painter's dream that will have you reaching for your camera.

If You Go:

Concord

Concord Museum	(978) 369-9609
Emerson House	(978) 369-2236
The Old Manse	(978) 369-3909
Minuteman Nat'l Historical Visitor Center	(978) 369-6993
South Bridge Boathouse	(978) 369-9438

The Wayside   (978) 369-6975

Lincoln
Lincoln Guide Service   (781) 259-1111
Codman House & Gropius House   (781) 259-8843
Decordova Museum   (781) 259-8355

Weston
For information about the **Case Estates**, call the Arnold Arboretum at (617) 524-1718.

The Rocky Coast:
Cape Ann & Environs

Rockport, Gloucester & Essex

A good name is sure to pique my curiosity, and the Welcome family's **Peg Leg Inn** on the waterfront in Rockport was no exception. I booked a night in one of the inn's 33 rooms, and enjoyed myself thoroughly. Besides the ocean views of Front Beach and Observatory Point, the Peg Leg also offers excellent seafood dinners in its on-site restaurant. Bring your own beer or wine, however. Rockport has been dry since 1856, the year Hannah Jumper and 100 other ax-wielding women smashed every bottle of liquor they could find!

I had a chance to talk with innkeeper Lillian Welcome (real last name) about her 22 years of operating the Peg Leg Inn. Neither she nor her husband Bob planned to become innkeepers. But when the Peg Leg came on the market, they felt the time was right to take the plunge. Though neither had innkeeping experience, Bob – a certified public accountant – knew the inn's track record from his work on its books.

Everything else they learned as they went along, thankful for help from staff that stayed on. Though they originally lived in what is now the main inn, the Welcomes later bought a house in town. Lillian believes that this move was a key to their success and longevity.

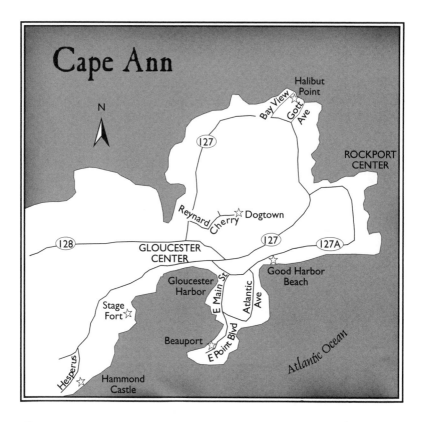

During my stay, I enjoyed **crystal-clear** weather. One sunny morning I took my cup of coffee out to the stone gazebo overlooking the rocky coast. Salt air seemed to have a calming effect. I took time to observe my surroundings, watching the gentle surf push strands of seaweed forward and then back, in an almost hypnotic motion. It was as if the waves were music and the seaweed was slowly dancing. Gulls went about their morning business, one repeatedly dropping a clam on the rocks to break its shell.

Later I followed a path behind the restaurant through **Millbrook Meadow**, the site of a grist mill in 1701. There, huge willow trees and King Crimson maples shade a small park and a set of children's swings. At the back of the park is the old mill pond where I spotted two young boys fishing. They had caught a bluegill but couldn't get the hook out of its mouth, so I offered to help. Though I've been fishing all my life, I think this was the first time I ever noticed just how beautifully colored the common bluegill is. Vivid blue on the gills, shades of golden brown on the flanks, and a patch of bright red. How lucky I was that these two young fishermen had helped me see things through the eyes of a child.

On the crest of a nearby hill stood a woman and her easel. The scene she was painting included a narrow lane with old homes to her right, and an old graveyard to her left. Straight ahead you could see the ocean over the various roof tops. Had the artist not been there, I might have walked right by this spot without fully realizing its beauty.

Making my way into the center of town, I saw dozens of specialty stores lining the road. I stopped and gazed at the rust-colored shack on **Bradley Wharf**. This is known as "Motif #1," because it is said to be the most painted view in the United States. But scenic vistas were everywhere, not just along Main Street.

I recommend "getting lost" by taking the backroads or following Route 127 along the water to **Halibut Point**. The state park here was once the site of a quarry operation, and interpretive signs help bring that history back to life. But, like the artists who flock to Rockport, I prized the park for its rugged ocean views. Trails lined by colorful vegetation led through granite blocks and boulders to the sea's edge. Here, I was content to doze in the sun.

Surf pounded the jumble of huge rocks that stretched along the coast as far as the eye could see. I picked my way down the path and rested just beyond the ocean spray. I watched a lobster boat that was bobbing on grey-blue swells stop just off shore. Oblivious to the rough conditions, the lobster man leaned over, pulled his traps from the depths, and then motored farther down the coast.

At **Halibut Point State Park** you can watch the waves and the boats, or just comb the beach. In spring, the park's trout lilies and violets please the eye, while autumn brings the golds and maroons of green briar, scrub oak, and bayberry. Summertime trips here make a nice break from the crowded beach. The views are tremendous – on clear days, one can see the New Hampshire coast and even Mount Agamenticus in Maine.

For over 100 years – beginning in 1840 – a quarrying operation cut granite from this coastal spot. Many signs of those early days are still visible, and a self-guided trail explains such quarrying terms as "dog holes" and "dead men." Initially, pieces of granite were hoisted from the quarry floor by massive derricks. These were powered by teams of oxen working block and tackle pulleys. Once lifted, the huge stone blocks were transported to a shed where cutters made a hole in the granite, then split it with a wedge. Finished blocks were used in such projects as the Holland Tunnel, The Brooklyn Bridge, and Boston's Custom House Tower.

Birders visit Halibut Point Reservation with regularity. Depending on the season, they might see a snowy owl, a peregrine falcon, a northern goshawk, or even an ivory gull. Experienced birders arrive just after dawn; they tend to favor the fall, when migrations of seabirds traverse the coast. Cormorants, scoters, common eiders, northern gannets, and common and red-throated loons all pass this way or take up winter residence. Fall is also the time for nor'easters, which can be spectacular to watch at Halibut Point.

The name "Halibut Point" originated with the early sailors, who had to "haul about" this massive point of rock. Most of our southern New England coastline is relatively flat and sandy, but Cape Ann's erosion-resistant granite bluffs more closely resemble Maine's shores than those of Massachusetts. This unique feature makes visiting here a real treat, quite different from other natural areas on the North Shore, such as Plum Island.

Humpback whales cruise the Atlantic just off the shore of Cape Ann, and a number of tour boats are available for whale-watching excursions. Cape Ann Whale Watch vessels boast a 99.5% sighting rate since 1979. Besides humpbacks, finbacks and right whales have also been spotted.

Smaller wildlife, such as birds, can be seen in salt water estuaries. The *Essex River Queen* explores these coastal waterways and also tours historic **Hog Island**. Be sure to bring your binoculars; you may spot a harrier hawk wheeling and diving as it hunts the marshlands.

Good birding is also possible along Island Road in Essex, a narrow country lane that parallels a salt marsh. In addition, Island Road is home to the **Stavro Reservation,** a glacial drumlin that can be climbed in 10 minutes. At the top of the hill you'll be rewarded with a view of the marsh, Hog Island, and the blue waters of the Atlantic beyond.

For those who wish to spend a weekend exploring the area, the **Old Farm Inn** is nestled on five acres of fields and woodlands adjacent to Halibut State Park. The farmhouse dates to 1799 and is filled with antiques. It's a quiet place removed from the bustle of downtown Rockport, yet close enough to visit the many art galleries, antique shops and restaurants for which the region is famous.

To tour the southern side of Cape Ann, take Route 127A south from Rockport Center along the ocean's edge. **Good Harbor Beach** – one of the Bay State's finest – is just beyond Rockport, in Gloucester. The half-mile beach has a rocky headland on one end, a small island that is accessible at low tide on the other, and a salt marsh protected by sand dunes. On my "research" trip there during the summer, I acted like a 16-year-old. I enjoyed surfing some big breakers on my boogie board, hooting and hollering with the rest of the kids. Only problem was, my body didn't have the resiliency of a teenager's. One wave in particular seemed out to get me. It picked me up on its crest, only to push me over its edge. I then went into a six-foot free-fall before the wave crashed on my back. It may have been my imagination, but I thought I heard a crack. I also know I felt one; when the foam of the wave deposited me in the shallows, I was amazed to find that I was still in one piece. It was exhilarating, exciting and invigorating. But after that, I avoided the really big waves and stuck with the stuff I could handle.

Good Harbor Beach

I stayed at Good Harbor from late afternoon into the evening – perhaps the best time to visit any beach. The crowds were gone, and the setting sun lit up the rocky point and the massive gray house perched at its edge, making for a most beautiful scene. With low tide, the beach had quadrupled in size, becoming almost two separate beaches. There was fine dry sand on the "permanent" beach, but the sand at the tidal portion was packed, making it the perfect place for a game of Frisbee. This lower beach was also noticeably cooler. At the southern end of the beach – near the rocky point – a tidal stream raced to the ocean. I watched three children have a ball in its shallow waters, chasing minnows and catching crabs. Is there anything finer than a warm summer evening at the shore?

Just beyond Good Harbor – near East Gloucester – is **Eastern Point**, a peninsula jutting southward to form Gloucester Harbor. For bicyclists, this is the place to go. Winding roads carry you along rocky coves, past spectacular mansions and through shaded woods. The best thing about this point of land is **Beauport**, a fantasy house/museum built by Henry Sleeper in the early part of the century. (Beauport is on Eastern Point Boulevard, a private road open to visitors only during museum hours in the warm weather months.)

I was immediately taken with Beauport's unusual design. There were archways, nooks and crannies, curves on the shingled roof, odd-shaped windows and chimneys, and enchanting courtyards with colorful flowers. The architecture is a blend of Queen Ann, Norman and Tudor styles; somehow, they all look perfect together. Having the ocean at your back door doesn't hurt, either.

Owner Henry Sleeper and local architect Halfdan Hanson first collaborated on the design of this house in 1907. Interestingly enough, neither man had any formal training in architectural design. Yet over the next 27 years, they continued adding to and improving the original home. Sleeper furnished the house with his unusual collection of European and American objects, as well as many "endangered" architectural features salvaged from abandoned New England homes dating back to the 18th century. He succeeded in creating a home that is full of surprises. Here he could delight famous guests such as John Astor, Helen Hayes, F. Scott Fitzgerald, Eleanor Roosevelt, and President William Howard Taft.

A tour through Beauport is not some dry, boring lesson in history and architecture. Rather, it's a fascinating walk through sheer creativity. Each room is very different from the last in terms of color, materials, furniture, and decorative touch. Some are dedicated to individuals Sleeper admired, while others speak to specific themes and different time periods. One room is outfitted with a hidden door. This led to a narrow stairway, where, it is said, the eccentric Sleeper would suddenly appear, dressed in a favorite costume to surprise his guests. Another room has a chapel theme, with a tiny cathedral ceiling, gothic windows, and fan-shaped shutters.

A large pine kitchen is decorated in an 18th-century vein, with a huge fireplace, Pennsylvania redware, and craftsmanship seldom seen today. Though many of the rooms are decorated in dark tones, the Golden Step Room is as bright as can be, with furniture painted robin's egg blue. It also features a huge window facing the ocean; this slides down into the wall, to admit the sea breezes. Another room that caught my fancy was the Round Book Tower, or circular library. Sleeper had the room built to accommodate a round bookcase he had discovered in Boston. The library has an upper floor with its own walkway. Hanging from one wall is an original Massachusetts state flag, made during the American Revolution. On another wall is an "Indian door" from Deerfield, Massachusetts. One side of the door has perpendicular planking, while on the other, the planks run diagonally. In between is a strip of rawhide. (This door was clearly designed to prevent Indians from hacking through it.) Also, pay close attention to the library's curtains – they are made out of wood.

It's easy to miss some of the smaller items, but be sure to ask questions about unfamiliar objects. Several rooms contained small glass balls. I learned that these were "witches' balls," used widely in the Boston area to ward off evil spirits. A beautiful configuration of colorful shells turned out to be a "sailor's Valentine." Sailors at sea would arrange the shells to look like roses and other flowers; they would give these tokens of affection to their sweethearts, when and if they returned. In the Octagon Room, you will notice that not only are there eight walls, but the dining table and rug are octagonal as well.

Beauport is not the only oddity on Cape Ann. Another is **Dogtown**, a ghost town with boulders that "speak." This lonely moor of land in the center of Cape Ann was once a thriving community. Local historians say that prior to the American Revolution, Dogtown was no different than the rest of New England, with God-fearing residents farming the bony soil. However, after the Revolution, coastal enterprises lured the settlers from Cape Ann's interior to its shores, leaving Dogtown to the very poor. The little settlement fell into disrepair, and those who continued to eke out a living there became more and more isolated from neighboring villages.

As time thinned Dogtown's remaining population, rumors of its transformation into a community of witches circulated around the Cape. Adding to the mystery was the pack of wild dogs that roamed the nearby woods, giving the town its name. (Once the pets of Dogtown residents, these dogs were left to run wild as their owners either died or were taken to the poorhouse.)

Today, Dogtown is a conservation area. Trails criss-cross the woods, passing forgotten cellar holes and glacial boulders as big as houses. Some of the smaller boulders are inscribed with mottoes extolling the virtues we should seek. These inscriptions were made at the behest of Roger Babson, a wealthy Gloucester native who purchased 1,000 acres of Dogtown in the early 1900s. (Babson was a financial wizard who predicted the stock market crash of 1929.) Some of the mottoes include admonitions such as "get a job," while others reflect Babson's entrepreneurial bent, with sayings such as "never try, never win."

Dogtown was a weird place, and still is.

Gloucester's waterfront no longer boasts huge commercial fishing fleets, but fishing and the ocean itself are still an important part of the town's economy. Besides the commercial fishing boats, there are a number of vessels that take visitors fishing, whale-watching, and sightseeing. An amphibious vehicle called *Moby Duck* takes guests through the streets of Gloucester and right into the sea, where it motors around like a power boat! Other vessels provide a variety of tours, ranging from a look at the region's lighthouses to a hands-on lobster hauling trip.

Just south of Gloucester on Route 127 is **Stage Fort Park**. Situated along the edge of Gloucester Harbor, this was the site of Gloucester's first settlement in 1623, just three years after the Pilgrims arrived at Plymouth. During the Revolution, the patriots erected a fort here; the actual cannons still point out at the harbor. Walkers will enjoy the park's ocean edge trail. Here, you can explore rocky outcroppings and read the commemorative plaques at historic points. You could also stop at the visitors' center to board a trolley that will take you from the park to the center of town.

Hammond Castle, off Route 127 on Hesperus Avenue, is another fascinating place to visit. The castle was built in the late 1920s by John Hays Hammond Jr., a millionaire inventor who once wrote, "For many years, I motored through Europe, collecting a piece of architecture that brought back the living presence of all ages. It is in the stones and wood that the personal record of man comes down to us. We call it atmosphere, this indescribable something that still haunts these old monuments. I have attempted to capture this in these walls and windows." True to his words, he did.

The replicated castle has everything a medieval lord might have had: twin towers, a drawbridge, leaded glass windows, fireplaces in every room, and gargoyles warding off evil spirits. Inside are Hammond's collections of early Roman, medieval, and Renaissance artifacts, along with an 8,200-pipe organ (the pipes are sunk two stories below the great hall, then rise eight stories in the towers.)

Perched on the edge of the ocean, the forbidding stone castle would appear to be a place where spirits linger. According to its caretakers, they do. Both individuals recalled hearing voices whispering, children laughing, and other strange noises at night – long after the castle has been closed to visitors. They also described feelings of being either welcome or unwelcome in a particular room, and sensing "presences" hovering nearby. Neither caretaker claims to have seen a ghost, but people who once rented the castle for a wedding swear they saw one.

If You Go:

Peg Leg Inn	(800) 346-2352
	(508) 546-2352
Old Farm Inn Bed & Breakfast	(508) 546-3237
Essex River Cruises	(508) 768-6981
Cape Ann Chamber of Commerce	(508) 283-1601
Rockport Chamber of Commerce	(508) 546-5997
Gloucester Tourism Commission	(800) 649-6839
Beauport	(508) 283-0800
Hammond Castle	(508) 283-7673

Cape Cod

Bicycling & Walking the Upper Cape

Woods Hole, West Falmouth, Bourne & Sandwich

It is still possible to find quiet spots on Cape Cod, especially if you visit before Memorial Day or after Labor Day. On a three-day weekend in October, I started out in Woods Hole, wound my way north along Buzzards Bay, then followed the Cape Cod Canal into Sandwich.

If you're like me, your impression of Woods Hole is only a fleeting one: this is where you catch the ferry to the islands. It wasn't until I actually spent a weekend at Woods Hole and talked to the locals that I learned this Falmouth village should be a destination rather than a pass-through. And summer isn't the only time to visit; the Cape is known for winters so mild that even its golf courses are open year-round.

Diana Smith, innkeeper of the **Marlborough Bed and Breakfast**, directed me to some of the beautiful natural areas scattered around Woods Hole. While talking over coffee and a hearty breakfast at the inn, I happened to mention that my bicycle was in the back of my old Subaru. She said that I was in luck; the **Shining Sea Bikeway** is apparently one of the best biking trails on the Cape.

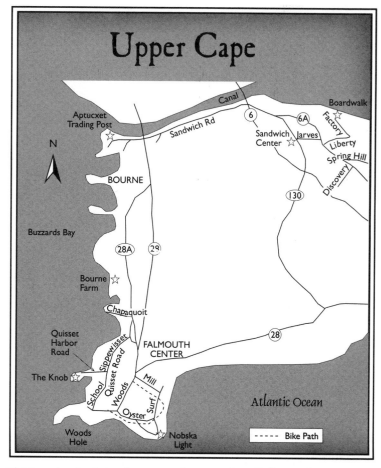

Thirty minutes later I was on the paved trail flying through oak woodlands on my way toward the ocean. Running from Falmouth center to Railroad Avenue, this bike path is about 3½ miles long. Because it is closed to motorized vehicles, a bicyclist has the freedom to enjoy a safe ride while soaking up the scenery. The trail emerges from the woods and passes by the **Oyster Pond Bird Sanctuary**, where wading birds, song birds and ducks are scattered over the pond and in the vegetation. After cruising by the ponds and marsh, you catch a glimpse of the ocean. Soon, the trail runs parallel to Surf Beach.

At Oyster Pond Road I turned off the trail, and, following Diana's advice, made a side trip up a hill to Fells Road. At the end of the road was **Sphors Garden**, a private garden that has been generously opened to the public. This is an enchanting place, with pathways winding through rhododendrons, azaleas, dogwoods, and blue spruce. Old ship's anchors – one from the *H.M.S. Bounty* – were placed along the trail, adding to the unique nature of the place. I made a mental note to return in April, when thousands of perennials (such as daffodils) bloom.

Upon reaching Woods Hole, I parked my bike, poked around a number of small shops, and enjoyed a cup of hot chocolate. Woods Hole has been said to have a "Harvard Square atmosphere," and that's a good description for it during the summer. But in the off-season, I found it a quiet village where everyone seemed somehow connected with the ocean – either through scientific research projects, ferry operation, or the fishing industry. It's a wonderful place to introduce children to the wonders of the marine world, with museums, aquariums and "discovery voyages" into Buzzards Bay.

Later, I visited what I consider the gem of the area. **The Knob** is a rocky point of land that juts out into Buzzards Bay. A trail leads from the parking area through twisted oaks and thick undergrowth, in a westward direction toward the open ocean. In 10 minutes, I crossed a narrow causeway and arrived at the Knob. The view was one of sparkling blue ocean, a lobster boat working its traps, and some impressive estates scattered along the mainland hills.

After soaking up the tranquility of the place, I headed back on the trail. On the way, I noticed an enormous white pine tree. Sometime in its youth, the tree's top had been broken off, forcing it to branch out low to the ground. Two rope swings hung from the upper branches. I shed my pack, prepared to swing. It took this old brain of mine a couple of minutes to realize that the only way to swing without a partner pushing, was to climb up a branch with the rope in my hand. Then, with the wooden seat between my legs, I pushed off and sailed wildly through the air.

Oh, the joy of it! I was a nine-year-old again, careening back and forth, a broad smile on my face. Should someone have come along the path at that moment, they would have thought me quite daft. Forty-year-old men just don't partake of these simple pleasures – or do they?

Heading north back towards the canal, I stopped at **Bourne Farm** in West Falmouth, off of Route 28A. The old farmstead has been well preserved, giving visitors a glimpse of the way Cape Cod used to look before rampant development swept through. The farmhouse and out-buildings sit on an open field above a marsh, with an orchard stretching out behind. Hiking trails criss-cross the property, passing woods of oak and cedar and following old stone walls.

While picnicking here I tried to visualize how the farm work was done in the 19th century. Clearing the fields was a monumental task – especially in New England, where the ground coughs up more rocks each spring. Stumps that needed pulling were left in the ground over the winter, where the frost loosened them. Then they were yanked out of the ground with a mallet lever attached to either a horse or an ox. On some farms, the stumps were pushed to the edge of the pasture and arranged in fence formation, with roots up. The root fences may have been unsightly, but they lasted longer than rail fences.

Another bit of history can be found at the **Aptuxet Trading Post Museum** in nearby Bourne. Inside this reconstructed Pilgrim trading post are period artifacts; Colonial stocks and a Dutch windmill are outside. It's a great spot to picnic, just a stone's throw from the southern end of the Cape Cod canal.

The seven miles of paved trails along the canal are perfect for traffic-free bicycling close to the salt water. I bike at a leisurely pace, stopping frequently to watch the surf casters angle for blues and stripers. **Mashnee Island** – just south of the canal, on Buzzards Bay – is another great place to take a spin on a bike. But my favorite stretch for pedaling purposes is near West Falmouth Harbor. Roads such as Chapaquoit Road and Old Dock Road will carry you past the bay, the salt marsh and handsome homes. I'll always remember my last outing there for the most colorful sunset I've ever seen. And for once, I had my camera to capture the moment. We all deserve one spectacular sunset a year; it has a way of uplifting the soul.

The next morning I went on to Sandwich, the Cape's oldest town. Located just over the Sagamore Bridge, it is best experienced by rambling down Route 6A – The Old King's Highway – and searching out the backroads. The center of Sandwich has the feel of an early settlement. Park your car and do your exploration on foot.

At the northern end of Shawmee Lake you will find **Dexter Gristmill**, a restored 17th-century water-wheel mill that still produces cornmeal. Adding to the charm of the town's center is the **Hoxie**

House. Built in 1637, it is the oldest house on Cape Cod. It, too, stands by the lake – just a few hundred feet south on Route 130.

One thing I'll always remember about the Hoxie House is how small its windows were. Glass was hard to come by in those times, and many a "window" was a pine slab that swung outward on leather hinges. When glass could be purchased, it was handmade, with ripples and bubbles. (At one time, a home with more than 10 panes was actually charged an extra tax.) People who could not afford glass panes sometimes used oiled paper or cemented rows of bottles in their window frames. These bottle windows didn't admit much light, but they were effective in stopping arrows!

Dexter Gristmill

Later in the 19th century, when glass became a bit easier to manufacture, Sandwich became known for its quality production. The **Sandwich Glass Museum** – also in the center of town – features displays of beautiful glass made here between 1825 and 1888. Nearby – inside the First Parish Meetinghouse (1833) – stands **Yesteryears Doll Museum**. This features antique dolls and doll houses from around the world. Across the street is the **First Church of Christ**, which dates to 1833 and gets my vote for the most handsome church on the Cape.

Grove Street, a scenic road lined with large maples, leads out of the town's center to the **Heritage Plantation**. This lush, 76-acre estate has a Shaker round barn that houses a number of antique cars, including Gary Cooper's 1931 Deusenberg. There are also Currier and Ives prints, a military museum and a working 1912 carousel. The property's gardens boast over a thousand varieties of trees and shrubs, with late spring being the best time to see the blooming rhododendrons and azaleas.

Heritage Plantation

On the bay side of Route 6A is an incredibly long boardwalk that spans a salt marsh and is superb for birding. The boardwalk's northern end looks out over Cape Cod Bay and the shoreline stretching off to the east. Before the Pilgrims touched down in the New World, explorers such as Captain Gosnold were charting these waters: "Neere this Cape we came to anchor in fifteen fadome, where we tooke great store of Codfish, for which we altered the name, and called it Cape Cod."

Spring Hill Road is one of the more scenic routes in the area, and ideal for bicycling. A quiet, narrow lane, it features fine homes, woods and a cranberry bog. The 1741 **Wing Fort House** is also here; tours are offered on weekdays in the summer. On the opposite side of Route 6A is Discovery Road. Another picturesque route, this is the site of the **Green Briar Nature Center**. Here are a colorful herb garden, a nature trail and natural history exhibits.

When it comes to biking on the Cape, remember two things: come in either the spring or the fall, and bring your camera.

If You Go:

Sandwich
Sandwich Glass Museum	(508) 888-0251
Yesteryears Doll Museum	(508) 888-1711
Hoxie House	(508) 888-1713
Green Briar Nature Center	(508) 888-6870
Wing House	(508) 888-1540
Heritage Plantation	(508) 888-3300

Falmouth
Bourne Farm	(508) 548-0711
Aptuxet Trading Post	(508) 759-9487

Woods Hole
Woods Hole Oceanographic Institute	(508) 548-1400
National Marine Fisheries Aquarium	(508) 548-5123
	(508) 548-7684
Ocean Quest	
(hands-on boating experience)	(508) 457-0508
Marine Biological Lab	(508) 548-3705
Marlborough Bed & Breakfast	(508) 548-6218

The Outer Cape: Dunes, Bike Trails & Pilgrims

Provincetown, Truro, Wellfleet & Eastham

On a warm autumn morning, my six-year-old daughter Kristin and I set out to explore the outer Cape, which Thoreau called "as wild and solitary as the Western Prairies used to be."

Gone was the summer traffic, and we breezed along Route 6, passing the scrub pines and oaks that hold this arm of sand together. After bypassing the "elbow" at Wellfleet, sand dunes started appearing near Truro. These signified that we were reaching our destination – Thoreau's wild land. The dunes were a light tan color, crested with rust-colored shrubs and sparse blades of tall green grass. Near a salt marsh where golden reeds waved in the wind we saw a great blue heron glide by, ghost-like and prehistoric-looking. This was why we had come to the Cape: to see the colors and wild creatures that make this outer desert so special.

Our plan was to bike the network of trails through the **Cape Cod National Seashore**. But before we did, I wanted to see the lay of the land, the ocean and the sky – all at once. The best place to obtain this kind of view was the tower of the **Pilgrim Monument** in Provincetown.

To reach the top of this 252-foot granite monument, you have to climb 116 heart-pumping stairs and 60 ramps. But the panoramic view is worth the effort. It is said that on a clear day one can even see the towers of Boston. Yet the most eye-catching vista is to the west, toward the dunes of Race Point. This is where we would be biking. Thoreau was right – the tip of the Cape certainly did look solitary.

At the **Province Lands Visitors Center** on Race Point Road, we scanned the exhibits and asked a ranger for his advice on the best biking trail. Without hesitation, he recommended the **Beech Forest Trail**.

Because it had few hills, this paved bike trail was indeed the perfect place for a beginner bicyclist to get in the swing of things. Kristin

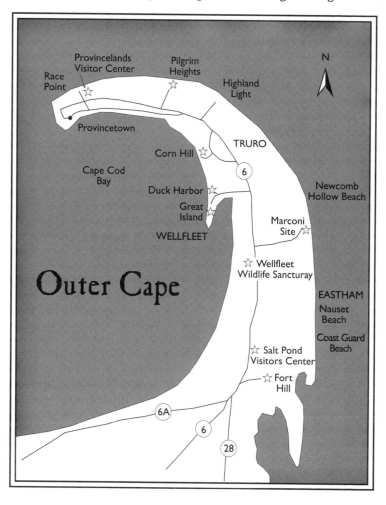

could cruise the relatively traffic-free path and enjoy the scenery at the same time. And I could do the same – without worrying about cars, because no motorized vehicles are allowed on these paths.

Biking a trail such as this gives you a real feeling of freedom, almost as if you are flying. No longer father and daughter, we became two kids out for adventure. "Why haven't I done this more often?" I asked myself.

We flew by beech, oak, scrub pines and even a few birch, soaking in the silence and the good feeling that comes from moving under your own power. Many of the beech trees still clung to their golden leaves. In one stretch, they even formed a colorful tunnel. This is the Cape Cod I have come to love, the season I prefer, and the means of travel that brings me the most joy.

After our legs grew weary, we drove to **Herring Cove Beach**. Here, we sat by the surf and munched on our sandwiches. I made the mistake of feeding crumbs to the nearby sea gulls, and within seconds more birds surrounded us. I compounded my mistake by walking back to the car for more bread. No sooner did I leave my spot in the sand, than a bold gull swooped down and grabbed my entire sandwich. Off it went, with lettuce, salami, and one slice of bread falling into the surf. Kristin could not stop laughing.

After the "great sandwich heist," we headed southward. Our first stop: **Pilgrim Heights**, where Myles Standish and other *Mayflower* passengers considered settling. Most people think that Plymouth Rock is the first place the Pilgrims landed in the New World. While Plymouth is the site of their first settlement, the Pilgrims didn't go there until they had spent a few weeks wandering around Cape Cod. Here, they had their first contact with the Indians. Had things transpired differently, Provincetown – not Plymouth – might have been their first settlement.

On November 11, 1620, the *Mayflower* anchored at what is now Provincetown. With winter approaching and provisions danger-ously low, Standish led an expedition of 16 well-armed men in search of food and fresh water. Not long after stepping on *terra firma*, they had their first encounter with local Indians.

Six natives were walking on the beach with their dog. Upon spotting the white men with their swords and muskets, they ran into the woods in fear. Standish and company gave chase. It is not clear why the Pilgrims pursued them; surely, it made a friendly meeting all but impossible. According to William Bradford (reputedly the author of *Mort's Relations*, a first-hand account of the Pilgrims), the newcomers chased the Indians"... to discover if there might be more lying in ambush."

The following day, the Pilgrims crossed into the interior of the peninsula and came upon a spring at what is now Pilgrim Heights. In Bradford's words, "Ye first New England water they drunke of and was, in their great thirste, as pleasante upon them as wine or beer had been in for-times." Finding baskets of corn buried under the sand, the Pilgrims promptly took all they could carry back to the *Mayflower*, reasoning that they would reimburse the natives at a later date. To make matters worse, some of the corn was taken from an area that may have been an Indian burial site.

Having found food and water, the Pilgrims considered settling here. They knew the fishing would be good, but worried about the water supply being insufficient come summer. Another concern was the shallow harbor. Bradford wrote of those who waded ashore in the frigid waters: "It brought most, if not all, coughs and colds, which afterward turned to scurvie, whereof many died."

Many on the ship wanted to travel farther north to a place the early explorers called Agoum (now Ipswich, Massachusetts). Others wanted to begin building immediately on Cape Cod. Instead, they decided more exploration was needed, wasting valuable time as winter closed in.

On December 6, 10 more armed men went ashore. During their two-day exploration of the coastline, they witnessed Indians carving up a dead whale. Again, the natives fled before contact could be made.

At dawn on the third day, the inevitable happened: "Indeans, Indeans – and withal their arrowes came flying amongst us." Amazingly, no Pilgrims were hit; nor were any Indians struck by the return musket fire.

This attack is what prompted the Pilgrims to sail to Plymouth. Here they found cleared fields, but no Indians. (Disease introduced by earlier explorers had wiped out scores of natives, including the tribe that had lived at Plymouth.) Finding this "a most hopeful place," the Pilgrims anchored here for good on December 26, 1620.

There is a marker at Cornhill, where Standish and his men first discovered the Indian corn. Kristin and I roamed the nearby back-roads, stopping at the **Bell Church** on Town Road. This is a fasci-nating hilltop church with a bell made by Paul Revere, miniature whale-shaped window latches, and Sandwich glass windows. An old graveyard surrounds the structure; it contains stones for the sailors lost at sea. One monument in particular reveals how young the mariners were. Most were in their 20s, while one victim was just a boy of 12.

Whenever I pass through Truro and Wellfleet, I can't help but think of Thoreau's trips to the Cape, which he chronicled in his book, *Cape Cod*. While walking from Eastham to Provincetown on three different visits, he became entranced by the power of the sea and the splendid isolation of the dunes. He wrote, "The solitude was that of the ocean and desert combined. A thousand men could not have seriously interrupted it, but would have been lost in the vastness of the scenery as their footsteps in the sand."

The wilds of Truro and Wellfleet still have the power to evoke such feelings. On the Atlantic side, take a walk beneath the dunes, from Newcomb Hollow Beach to White Crest Beach. Or explore the gentler bay side, where the vistas are equally impressive. In the evening, Kristin and I visited **Duck Harbor Beach** (or "Sunset Beach"). Here we witnessed a most spectacular sunset, made all the more breathtaking by the undulating dunes. The barren scene recalled a moonscape, with an open, spacious feel not often found in New England. We sat on the crest of a mountain of sand and let the colors roll past; reds, pinks, oranges, and even purples spread over the western horizon. I thought of the closing line in Thoreau's book: "A man may stand there and put all America behind him."

Kristin and I spent a comfortable night at the **Top Mast**, a resort motel situated on Cape Cod Bay in Truro. The ocean was just 50 feet beyond our picture window. After a late dinner, we went down to the beach, with a million stars shining overhead. There is something special about a night on the beach; other senses besides sight take over. The salt air and the gentle lapping of the surf have a therapeutic, almost hypnotic power. We could see the outline of the beach, but little else. My imagination took over, and I visual-ized giant striped bass cruising the shallows. I took a few casts with my surf rod, hoping that a striper would hear my plug splash down and turn to attack. Sometimes you can combine visualiza-tion with positive thinking and perhaps manifest an outcome. But on that dark night, it was not to be.

After a half-hour of walking the beach, the chill in the air sent us back to the warmth of our room. Kristin immediately fell into that deep sleep with which all children are blessed. I entertained myself reading a book entitled *"From Time and Town: A Provincetown Chronicle,"* by Mary Heaton Varse. We may think that Provincetown just recently become "different" but, according to Varse, "Provincetown from its earliest days has been freer, richer in life than its neighbors. Back in 1727, Truro asked to be severed from Provincetown because of the goings-on there."

In the morning, we had breakfast with Al Silva, who with his wife Nancy owns the Top Mast. Both are natives of Provincetown. For a brief period, they lived and worked in the Boston suburbs. But with the Cape in their blood, they were destined to return – which they did 24 years ago, when they bought the hotel. I think they hold the record for a husband and wife team who not only work together, but have built a distinctive business that attracts vacationing families year after year. The first few years were tough, and there were some sleepless nights, but now they look back and realize their choice was the right one. "Every night, I look over the bay, and somehow the sunset is just a little different than the night before," Al said.

After breakfast, Kristin and I followed North Pamet Road to a hiking trail on Truro's national seashore that is nothing short of spectacular. A trail winds through shaded woodlands, then skirts a pond before intersecting with a boardwalk spanning an old cranberry bog. Beyond a weathered barn, a narrow foot trail passes by huge dunes covered with vegetation. Just beyond is the Atlantic. We soon crested the final dune, which ended abruptly in a cliff overlooking the shoreline. We sat there, mesmerized by the sweeping vista of ocean, beach and rolling dunes.

I remember thinking how even the light during autumn seems finer and the air clearer than in summer. Thoreau, too, loved autumn on the Cape. He wrote, "I suspect that fall is the best season, for then the atmosphere is more transparent, and it is a greater pleasure to look out over the sea. In autumn, even in August, the thoughtful days begin, and we can walk anywhere with profit."

Henry Beston, author of *The Outermost House*, also began his Cape Cod odyssey in autumn: "I went there to spend a fortnight in September. The fortnight ending, I lingered on, and as the year lengthened into autumn, the beauty and mystery of this earth and outer sea so possessed and held me that I could not go. The world to-day is sick to its thin blood for lack of elemental things, for fire before the hands, for water welling from the earth, for air, for the dear earth itself underfoot. In my world of beach and dune these elemental presences lived and had their being... "

Somehow, the Cape seems more real during the autumn – more beautiful, as if the land tolerates the hordes of summer visitors, but saves its best side for those who linger. The bird migrations peak in the fall and, if you're lucky, you'll see butterflies drifting over the dunes. Beston described his sightings of monarch butterflies as "... one of the strangest and most beautiful of the migrations. Their movements were as casual as the wind, yet there was an unmistakable southerly pull drawing them on."

During October on the Cape, there are days filled with the grace and tranquility of butterflies, as well as days of savage storms with windswept breakers pounding the exposed beaches of the Cape's forearm. At the Marconi site in **Wellfleet** – where Guglielmo Marconi sent the first wireless message across the Atlantic in 1903 – there is an observation platform that affords a 360° view. On a fall day, you can feel the wind, smell the salt, and see the subtle autumnal tints of the dunes stretch out to the dark Atlantic.

Wellfleet Sailboats

I once walked this stretch of beach and noticed something was moving in the water next to me. It was a seal, cruising mostly underwater in about two feet of water, heading in the same direction I was. It showed not the slightest concern for my close proximity. Other trips to this area have yielded equally bizarre sights. Most memorable was a bluefish blitz. These toothy predators – each about two feet long – were slashing through the surf, making the water boil in spots just offshore. They were in a feeding frenzy, having encircled their prey (menhaden or "pogies"). The sight was truly incredible. Beston described seeing a similar sight on a moonlit night, when "... the whole churn of sea close off the beach vibrates with a primeval ferocity and intensity of life; yet is this war of rushing mouth and living food without a sound save for the breaking of the seas." He reported seeing thousands of sand eels beaching themselves, and later spotted the predators themselves – dogfish, some of which the surf flung up and stranded on shore!

On the bay side of Wellfleet are two wonderful walking trails. **Great Island** is a sandy point of land that forms Wellfleet Harbor. Intrepid walkers can take an eight-mile round-trip route through shrub dunes, pitch pine and tidal flats to **Jeremy Point** (which can only be reached during low tide). Because Great Island is large, it's the perfect place to play the castaway, combing the beach on a deserted island.

Another great spot to explore is **Wellfleet Bay Wildlife Sanctuary**, which is where Kristin and I made a short stop to walk the salt marsh. Birding is excellent here, with herons, egrets, and other wading birds often seen. Those of you interested in the Cape's plant life should attempt the **Goose Pond Trail**, a self-guiding nature walk about 1½ miles long. Kristin and I used the trail booklet to help us identify plants we have passed hundreds of times but never recognized.

Perhaps the most beautiful scene on all the Cape is at **Fort Hill**, just off Route 6 in Eastham. This small hill slopes to the east, overlooking fields, salt marshes and an estuary protected by the Cape Cod National Seashore. If you're vacationing on the Cape and you want to see a truly memorable sight, go to Fort Hill at dawn. The land awakens to soft colors, bird calls, and tranquility itself. Then you have the whole morning to get out and explore, with the afternoon free to snooze on the beach.

If You Go:

Pilgrim Monument	(800) 247-1620
	(508) 487-1310
Province Lands Visitor Center	(508) 487-1256
Wellfleet Bay Wildlife Sanctuary	(508) 349-2615
The Top Mast	(508) 487-1189

Author's Note

It's fitting that I write this final note on pad and paper, while sitting deep in the woods. A nuthatch is investigating a nearby tree and a red squirrel chatters to warn me that this is his section of forest. Clouds sail overhead; it's good to lie back and watch them through the hemlocks.

I am occasionally asked if I worry about ruining places by writing about them. On the surface, this would seem to be a real dilemma, but over time I've realized that the positives outweigh the negatives. People who venture on the backroads are the kind of people who respect the land. Repeat visits to special places can actually make a person love the land, and you protect what you love.

Massachusetts is one of the country's most densely populated states; yet if you've explored the locations in this book, you would never know it. The open spaces, natural beauty and public access are there because individuals cared. Some of these spots reflect the positive efforts of state government, while others are the work of organizations such as the Massachusetts Audubon Society or The Trustees of Reservations. The remainder are simply gifts from people who passed up personal profit to save what matters.

We can do our part by taking the time to protect the earth. At some point, all of us will be presented with an opportunity to help. You will know when it's the right time to step up to the plate and make a difference.

These quiet places help balance me, offering the solitude so necessary to refresh. I'm convinced that they keep me healthy, and more than once I've felt my spirit soar. Thank God for quiet places.